THE LONG RUN

* * *

My Son's Inspired Journey Through
Traumatic Brain Injury

by Annette Whitlock

All artwork created by Jonathan Whitlock
To see more of his work and to listen to his 1998 recording of "The Long Run," go to
www.jonathanwhitlockart.com

Printed in the United States of America

First Printing: July 2018
KDP Amazon

ISBN-13: 978-1-981-05157-1

*To all the caregivers
that lovingly, faithfully serve those with disabilities.*

CONTENTS

INTRODUCTION

* * *

Admittedly, I am amazed at just how well we handled those most trying years of our lives from 1999-2002. I haven't always handled difficulties as well. I suppose we absolutely knew that we needed to include God in this one. That was the key. And yet, how many books or movies have you read or seen that nothing is mentioned of a spiritual nature even though most people believe in a higher power?

Despite my professional lack of experience, I wanted to write this book to let you know what it's like using God, that Higher Power, through whatever crises you might face. It doesn't have to be a traumatic brain injury. It doesn't even have to be a life-threatening experience. God will be there for you in the details of your life if you but ask. Why? Because He loves you.

The Long Run

PROLOGUE

* * *

In the arms of the angel
Fly away from here
From this dark cold hotel room
And the endlessness that you fear
You are pulled from the wreckage
Of your silent reverie
You're in the arms of the angel
May you find some comfort here

– "ANGEL" WORDS & MUSIC BY SARAH MCLACHLAN

May , 1999; Southern Virginia College at Buena Vista, VA. From 18-year-old Jonathan Whitlock's letter to Melissa Brubaker:

I'm not sure I can stay here long. Something creeps up on me like an approaching waterfall on a river. It's like somehow I'm being warned of some drastic turn my life is about to take. Perhaps not drastic... just change. This much I know – there is a task I must serve. I cannot imagine how it would; I feel totally unprepared and inadequate. This is why I feel some change would be drastic....

Everything I do seems suddenly, strangely significant (pardon the alliteration), as if someone was watching closely. I find immense symbolism in everything I do or create. Nothing seems coincidental.... Pulls are very extreme, as in I feel very strongly I should stay and also very strongly I should leave.

You know, looking and reading back over this, it all seems very stupid, and I shouldn't give it a second thought. But my name is being called over and over again. I know it is being called by something or someone much more powerful than me. I know something is going to happen very soon.... When we are told something will happen soon... we are given a knowledge of its existence, and a warning to prepare.

March 7, 1999 ; Lancaster, PA. From 39-year-old Annette Whitlock's journal :

Jonathan was able to come home again last weekend since they had Monday off. The weekend before that, he had quite an amazing and spiritual experience. He was finding himself slipping into depression again, but this time he asked a couple of good friends of his to give him a priesthood blessing*. In that blessing, he was blessed to be healed and that the darkness would go away for a time....

Jonathan gained two very important things from this blessing. He actually felt the darkness depart and his mind clear. He understands that this cloud over his mind has been lifted even though the problems may still exist. However, he can now think much clearer and know all thoughts are his. He now feels in control. And secondly, what a lift to his self-esteem these words were. Truly, they are quite powerful words! He certainly now knows his mission in life counts for something and that his Father in Heaven has a purpose and a love for him.

At first, this was all hard for me to fathom. But as it begins to sink in, I have to ask myself, "Why not?" Why wouldn't the priesthood power be able to heal him? Why wouldn't Jonathan have such a strong mission in life? He certainly has been blessed with a keen intelligence, many talents, and a strong legacy of faith.

Since then, we have spoken briefly about the experience. He mentioned that on the way home to PA, he began to feel the darkness come over him again, but he was able to not let *it take a hold of him. I encouraged him to pray just as soon as he feels it coming on. I also reminded him that Satan knows just as well his mission and will fight just as hard for his soul.*

It was good to see Jonathan in person. He does seem more at peace with himself.... The other thing Jonathan expressed to us is how much he loves and appreciates us. It's so good to hear such loving words and be the recipient of his bear hugs!

*Indicates words that are found in the Glossary of Mormon Terms found at the end of the book.

March 14, 1999. *Update on Jonathan: He's doing really well, despite having a nasty cold all week that put him out of classes and behind with all of his responsibilities. He got very little sleep as well. Surprisingly, all this hasn't brought him down mentally. That was some powerful blessing! We'll get to see him and Megan Dalton in about a week and a half for Easter break. I'm looking forward to taking them back so I can see Jonathan's paintings before he sells them all. Actually, that's a little bit of an exaggeration. However, he has already sold two to fellow students and is in the process of selling two more to his art teachers. Now, if his art teachers are willing to pay him ($100 and $200 each!), my son truly must be more than just a good artist. Isn't that cool? Who knows, I could be raising a future Picasso. I've always wanted to write a book − just didn't know it would be a biography on* *my famous son! I write this tongue in cheek, but still I wonder... what does the future hold?*

May 22, 1999; Letter to extended family.

Hello Family –

This is the kind of stuff that I would share with you if you were here in Lancaster. Being family, you'll understand.

First, Jonathan and his very dear friend, Melissa Brubaker, took a trip down to Lexington, Virginia to visit friends and the art gallery where his show is. He came back with the news that he sold one of his paintings to a businessman for $700! My first thought was, "If someone is willing to spend that much money on an unknown artist, perhaps we're not the only ones that think he's a good artist!

Secondly, I got an interesting phone call the other day. Remember me telling you about getting accepted to perform in the Strasburg "Kaleidoscope of Talent" show? I was planning to sing "Steal Away" until one of the ladies in charge called and asked if I could sing Sarah McLaughlin's "Angel." Apparently Jim, one of the other judges was impressed with the way I sang and kept telling her that he would love "the girl, Annette Whitlock" to sing it for that night. Gladys told him that it wouldn't be fair to me, but he kept bringing it up whenever they talked about the talent show. In fact, the last time she saw Jim he mentioned it again. Then on Tuesday he was killed by a drunk driver. They'll be dedicating the evening to him and wanted me to say a few words about how he felt and why I was singing this song. What an experience this will be to sing such a song for someone who had no idea he was going to be taken. How I hope he'll be listening! I went today to find the music. All they had was a simple version, but fortunately Jonathan had already figured out much of the song on the piano when it first came out by simply listening to it on the tape. He's reluctant to play, but he's the only way I'll be able to do this. Thank goodness for such a talented son!

June 6, 1999; Sunday night, 11:48 p.m. *Oh, how I love Sundays! Especially ones like today where there's enough time to----*

Well, that was a nice thought. It's 2 ½ hours later. Let's see.... what took me away? Ah yes, Peter was ready for bed, which is our cue to have family scripture and prayer. Then we read an article from The Friend*. Then Mom called. Then Jeff and I got into a deep discussion about his work situation. Then Jonathan and I got into a discussion about spiritual prep for his mission*. And voila – it's almost midnight.

Top: Jonathan hanging out in the art room at SVU with Melissa Brubaker & fellow students Will Woolsten & Megan Dalton. Bottom: Whitlock family April, 1999 – Lauren (12), Jonathan (18), Peter (8), Andrew (16), Annette (39), Jeff (42)

PART I

The Hospital

* * *

Quitting has its season but it's not in my
air today.
No, today's the day for keeping on and for
seeing it through, they say.
It's the season of small victories and of
battles fought and won.
Yes, today will be filled with battles;
some are welcomed, others shunned,
In the long run.

– "THE LONG RUN" WORDS BY MARK KUNKEL,
JONATHAN'S UNCLE;
MUSIC BY JONATHAN WHITLOCK

CHAPTER 1

June 14, 1999; Monday morning, 3:04 a.m. *It's what every parent dreads — that late night phone call from the hospital. But when it happened, it took me awhile to register why a "Michael from Lancaster General Hospital" was calling at 1:07 a.m. Even when he told Jeff that our son, Jonathan, had been in a car accident and could he come down to the emergency room, the seriousness of it all still didn't register, especially since all he said was that Jonathan was going under "diagnostic testing." So while I waited for Jeff's phone call from the hospital, I wrapped myself up in blankets in bed (I get cold when I'm scared) and tried to think positive thoughts.*

1:40 a.m. *Jeff calls with the news that Jonathan has a skull fracture and a broken right leg, and that he's stable but unconscious. They are currently taking CAT scans. Nothing yet about the accident except that he was the only one brought in. I lie there in bed sending silent prayers upward for Jonathan. It occurs to me that I also need to pray that Jeff and I will be prepared for what lies ahead. Why would I think* *that, I wonder? I finish reading the Ensign*. Just as I doze off, another phone call.*

2:30 a.m. This time Jeff is able to give me a clearer picture. Jonathan is currently in surgery to have a blood clot removed from his brain. If possible, they will try to also operate on his leg. This should take about 1 ½ hours. There is significant brain swelling, but they're not sure at this point if there will be temporary or permanent damage. We should expect him to be in the hospital for 5-10 days.

Jeff was able to see him. He's still unconscious and pretty banged up... two black eyes, lacerations, and hooked up to a breathing mechanism. I listen to all of this not quite knowing what to think or feel. I keep asking questions.

The accident happened between 12 and 12:30 a.m. on US 222. He was on his way home from dropping off his good friend Melissa after picking her up from work and talking late as they usually do. Melissa happened to be in a car accident about the same time last night when she fell asleep at the wheel on the way home from being out with Jonathan. She totaled her car when she hit a mailbox, but fortunately received only cuts and bruises. Apparently as Jonathan was on his way home tonight, he slid on the wet road (it had been misting) and slammed into a telephone pole on the driver's side. Unfortunately, he wasn't wearing his seat belt and it appeared that he was speeding as he came to the curve in the road. The state trooper said he won't receive a citation.

Apparently in such trauma cases, they realize we don't need this added burden. "Raul," the '90 Mitsubishi Mirage we bought less than a month ago for the boys to use is totaled. So is the telephone pole and part of an Amish man's fence. Someone heard the accident and called the police. They had to cut the roof and door open to remove our son. They then helicoptered him in to Lancaster General.

I ask Jeff if he has had a chance to give Jonathan a priesthood blessing*. Not yet, but he hopes to when he's done in surgery. Should I come? It wouldn't do much good. Just pray. Pray for our son.

2:42 a.m. *This time I kneel at my bedside and pray vocally. As I try to, it's difficult to get the words out. I'm still feeling numb. I ask for the Lord to guide the doctor's hands and instruments. I pray that Jonathan will have the mental and physical strength to get through this. Then the thought comes clearly to me. "Part of a plan. This is all part of a plan, Annette." I vocally spell out this plan as I receive it. "Jonathan is in the Lord's hands. Lessons will be learned, particularly lessons on obedience. This all needs to take place to get Jonathan where he needs to be." And somehow Melissa is connected in all of this. I continue to pray. I thank my Heavenly Father for such a man as Jeff by my side. How grateful I am for his priesthood power and strength of character. I trust my husband. I trust my Father.*

I begin to cry for the first time as I picture telling friends and loved ones the news. It also occurs to me that Jonathan won't be sending his mission papers in next week. Guess I better cancel the appointments for his physical. Oh yes, and the one with the bishop* on Tuesday. What insurance do we get for him after he turns 19 on July 2nd? I realize at this point that sleep won't come any time soon, so I decide to head downstairs and write in my journal. As I turn on the lights and the computer, I see things all around me of Jonathan's. I get teary all over again. Somehow, I think we won't forget Jeff's birthday when he turned 43 and got that call from the hospital.

CHAPTER 2

*J*une 14; Monday morning, 5:41 a.m. *After getting less than an hour's sleep, it takes me a little longer to orient myself when the phone rings. Jeff lets me know that the doctor is done operating. The good news is that the blood clot was between the skull and membrane and not between the membrane and brain. Also, the skull fractures are such that he won't need any metal plates. The bad news is that there is blood in the lungs that he swallowed so he'll probably develop pneumonia. When I asked Jeff if he was able to give him a blessing, he said he did. But when he tried to describe it, he broke down and sobbed, something I rarely have seen him do. I know at that point I need to go in. Jeff says he'll pick me up.*

6:00 a.m. *After waking Andrew [Jonathan's 16-year-old brother] and telling him what is going on, Jeff and I leave for the hospital. We talk. We go over all the details. Jeff tries to prepare me for how bad Jonathan looks. Despite this, I break down and sob when I see my son in such horrible shape. His head is swathed in bandages with bleeding showing through-. His left leg is in traction with a pin through the* knee. His eyes are swollen with the lids a deep purple – apparently a normal reaction to the swelling and bleeding. There are at least five monitoring tubes he's hooked up to. We stay for an hour wondering where this will all lead.

9:30 a.m. Jeff and I are back in the hospital. While at home, we told all the kids what was happening and knelt together in prayer. We make necessary phone calls, i.e. the family doctor, insurances, Jon's work, Jeff's work. The hardest ones are to Jeff's parents and Bishop* Swavely. My parents aren't home.

Back at the hospital, we finally begin to sense the seriousness of the situation with the doctor and nurse saying such things as "he's not responding as we hoped" and "prepare for weeks in the hospital, a year of rehab." When they leave, I ask Jeff the question hanging in the air, "Could he die?" We talk about the possibility of his life hooked to a machine. We pray together. We cry together. We remember the blessings he has been promised and we hope.

Our emotional roller coaster ride begins when Jonathan begins to move his body, obviously in pain. Jeff and I plead for him to come back, but soon the movements cease. The nurse is so kind and caring. How difficult it must be to be a nurse on this trauma floor. She encourages us to talk to him, touch him, direct him. They still don't know if this helps, but as long as there is a chance that it does, we'll do it.

12:15 p.m. *Marty Bennett just called. What a dear friend as well as Relief Society* President. Meals are already coming in. Phone calls are being made for a special fast* among ward* members. How much has changed in just 12 hours! You truly never know when it's your turn to experience such a heart rending, life threatening experience.*

2:40 p.m. *I come to the waiting room while they clean his room. I lie down and end up napping for 40 minutes. When I awake, I see a Mennonite family also in the waiting room. We begin to talk and find out that we have very much in common. The mother tells me her 16-year-old twin boys were in a car accident Wednesday. The one is released, but the other is across the room from Jonathan with the same diagnosis. They give me hope as they tell about the little improvements their Willie has made each day. I see that she, too, is keeping a journal. Must be a mother thing.*

2:50 p.m. *Cathy, the social worker, joins us in the waiting room. I have a wonderful conversation with her as I see that she's a great resource to have. She wants to know about Jonathan and his family.*

I then call Melissa. She reminded me that this all happened to her dad three years ago. She'd like to come down and the staff gave their okay. I hope I'll be here.

7:00 p.m. *Just had a wonderful flood of visitors from the ward. What a wonderful support system! Also saw the trauma doctor. This time she mentioned organ donation as a* *possibility down the road. She's not a "doomsday doctor;" just helping us prepare for the worst while hoping for the best. Heading home now....*

CHAPTER 3

Come, little child, and together we'll learn
Of his commandments, that we may return
Home to his presence, to live in his sight
Always, always to walk in the light.

- "TEACH ME TO WALK IN THE LIGHT" HYMN
#304, VERSE 2; WORDS BY CLARA W. MCMASTER.
FROM HYMNS OF THE CHURCH OF JESUS CHRIST OF
LATTER-DAY SAINTS (AS ARE ALL OTHER HYMNS)

June 15; Tuesday afternoon, 3:00 p.m. *So much to catch up on. Before I headed home last night, that wonderful group of visitors I mentioned knelt in prayer with Jeff and me right there in the waiting room. I don't think I'll ever forget that scene or the feelings I had as Bishop*

Swavely prayed. I truly feel strength as well as love surrounding me.

Lauren and Peter [Jonathan's siblings, age 12 and 9 respectively] spent_the night at the Woolstenhulme's, members of the church who live nearby, since we're still not sure who is spending the night at the hospital. The kids are glad to see me. The house is straightened. Children have been sweet to each other. I talk to my mom and dad, brothers and sister. The emotion is pretty numb. Both Jeff and I start to feel the effects of little sleep. Jeff calls his dad. Can you come tonight and give Jonathan a blessing with me? Of course. He and Mom W. show up at 10:30 from Frederick, Maryland, two hours away. When we arrive back at the hospital, Stake* President Arnold and his wife are there, as well as John Hume. How sweet! Mom and I go in to see Jon. It shakes her up pretty badly to see her oldest grandchild in such sad shape. But I'll always remember the closeness we felt. After getting Jonathan re-bandaged and cleaned up, Jeff and Dad give the blessing. Dad directs Jonathan to choose the Lord's will despite how enticing the other side must be. Back in the waiting room, the priesthood brethren encircle around me as Jeff gives me a blessing, then Dad gives Jeff a blessing. I was glad to hear Jeff remind me of the close bond Jonathan and I have always had.

All leave after midnight and I head over to the other waiting room to get some sleep. 3:15 I am awakened by a phone call. Thad Rittenhouse would like to visit. Despite my somewhat stupored stage (which he profusely apologized for), I enjoy the visit and chance to discuss spiritual things with this friend from the ward.

I get four more hours of sleep until I awake at 8:30. Back at home, I try to change in between fielding more phone calls of love and concern. Andrew and I go pick up the milk at the farm, then he drops me off at the hospital where Jeff has been sitting with Jonathan. [Now looking back, I wonder how I could allow my 16-year-old son to get in a car and drive? Oh yes, I am a trusting individual!] *Jeff has been close to or in tears much of today while I have settled into a calm, comforting mood. Jeff shares his feelings with me. I particularly cherish his words, "I will rejoice no matter the outcome, for it will be the Lord's will." I, too, feel that way. We read some beautiful scriptures together. We both sense a power of faith that must be coming from all the prayers and fasting on our behalf. I sing to Jonathan "I Am a Child of God" and "Teach Me to Walk." How did I ever get through that?*

12:30 p.m. *Lunch is brought in by dear sisters* from the ward. What a huge feast! Melissa and the Elders* also stop by. Jeff and I enjoy simply munching and visiting with them. Jonathan's condition has changed very little. His lungs are clear with no more threat of pneumonia, good news we freely pass on to others.*

7:15 p.m. *I take Lauren to Mutual*. It was going to be a pool party, but because of the effect all this has had on the kids, they end up at the church. I take the opportunity to reassure, update, and testify. And hug. Oh, what wonderful, warm hugs!*

9:00 p.m. *Jeff and I run into the Johnstons outside the hospital. We have a great visit with these friends of ours. Tracey promised – just as she did when Peter was born – spaghetti and paper plates when all the fuss dies down. It felt good to be outside on such a beautiful evening.*

11:00 p.m. *Jeff and I kneel beside Jonathan to pray with him. Just before Jeff closes with the words, "Help him to submit to Thy will," Jon has a really bad episode that shoots all the stats way high. We wonder if this is a sign..... I think I'll stay one more night.*

CHAPTER 4

June 16; Wednesday afternoon. *Jonathan ended up having three more of these episodes during the night. They now have to keep him constantly on morphine and some kind of paralysis drug. Meanwhile, I slept uninterrupted for seven hours. I awoke, however, feeling drained. I took a half-hour nap in my own bed this morning which did wonders. I think I'll sleep in my own bed tonight. At home, seeing Jonathan's favorite orange afghan made me cry, but other than that, I've been near tears but okay. It looks like I won't be able to have my precious one-on-one time with Jonathan today. He's needing constant care from the nurse.*

June 17; Thursday afternoon. *Last night during my visit home, Peter and Lauren said some interesting things. Peter came up to me at the dinner table with a concerned look on his face and said, "Mom, I have a funny feeling inside. I'm thinking maybe I shouldn't pray for Jonathan to get better fast." I then told him what we're praying for – that Jonathan will be strong enough to do what the Lord wants, and that he will not have to suffer too much. Peter was relieved at* hearing that. For a nine-year-old, he's a perceptive child through all of this; not consumed, but obviously concerned.

Later that evening, my Lauren and I were sitting on the front porch when she told me about a dream she had Sunday, the night of the accident. She said that in the dream, Jonathan came to her and told her that something bad was going to happen to him, even that he might die. That was it. She also mentioned that that is why she felt so weird when she was told about the accident. Why would she have this dream? Was it the Lord preparing her for the long, upcoming ordeal?

Last night was my first night in my own bed. What a good night's sleep! Jonathan had a good, stable night – so much so that they were able to move him to a fancier bed and a larger room. He also got another CT scan done this morning and he was able to get his fractured femur operated on. They've put a rod through his thigh that will more than likely stay there. Yay, no cast! Since the operation, his ICP (inter cranial pressure) is much lower, probably indicating how much his broken leg was hurting him.

Mom W. left today with Peter and Lauren until Saturday. I'm going to miss them, but I'm thinking they'll enjoy the change of scenery. Andrew stayed back to work. I'm settling into my new life here.

June 18; Friday afternoon. Today I sense the routine that will follow for the next few days, weeks... months? I was *getting cold so I went outside and found a beautiful solitary garden to stretch out, finish reading, and soak in the light. I hate to miss these pleasant June days.*

Andrew came back with us again last night. He was able to have alone time with his brother. When I came in, I noticed the tears were close to the surface of this 16-year-old son of ours. He said he really misses Jonathan, especially hearing his voice.

Some of our neighbors got together their money with Tina Reese going out and buying at least a week's worth of groceries for us! I was so touched by this unselfish kindness. These kinds of things are what bring me to tears.

CHAPTER 5

June 19, 1999; Saturday

Hello dear friends and family:

I thought I would periodically try and give you an update on Jon's condition via email. If you know of any other email addresses that you would like me to include, just let me know. We have received such strength from your concern, love, service, and prayers. I know that Jonathan would be a little overwhelmed with all this attention on him. It's great! I also appreciate any of your notes. I take them in and read them to him.... They also touch my heart.

Last night they put Jonathan in a drug-induced coma and will keep him that way for 3-4 days. They're hoping that this will keep his brain calm so that the swelling can go down. It just didn't go down after that crucial 72-hour period, but they still have a few ideas left. Unfortunately, he won't be able to respond during this time. Yet if we can get his ICP number down, then we can get an MRI and see what damage was done to the brain stem and possibly the brain.

This morning was the first time I didn't go immediately back to the hospital with Jeff. I've spent a few hours here cleaning bathrooms and taking out Jon's garbages for him. (That was his Saturday chore.) It's been rather therapeutic, but I'm anxious to see him, so will close.

Know that there continues to be a peace of mind that we feel so strongly that I know can only come from a loving and caring Father in Heaven as well as from all your prayers. May your testimonies continue to be strengthened as ours have from this ordeal.

With love,

Annette

June 21; Monday morning. *Yesterday was a rather difficult day for me emotionally. We decided to go to church as a family. We have felt such strength from two sources – God and His saints – that it just seemed a natural thing to have all three entities come together in His house. I was fine until the opening hymn which was "O My Father" [LDS hymn #292], one of Jeff's and my favorite songs to sing to Jonathan. The tears shed in Sacrament Meeting* were sweet tears, however. I was a bit more settled by Young Women* so I was able to give my lesson.*

I talked to Mom and Dad last night. Mom mentioned that they would come and get the kids the day before they leave for the family reunion and then stay a few days after. It was very difficult to suggest that they might want to come sooner just in case Jonathan's not here when they get back. To verbalize the stark reality of the situation to someone with such hope for his recovery... I broke down and cried when I talked to both of them. I suppose there's still a part of me that needs to just be their little girl.

Megan Dalton, Jon's best friend from Southern Virginia College, came up Saturday night. I felt that Melissa needed her strength. Thank goodness these two dear friends of Jon's became fast friends this past year. Melissa shared a part of a letter that Jonathan wrote to her about a month ago. She's going to bring it in for us to look at today, but from what Megan said, Jonathan wrote that he felt that something life changing was going to happen to him and that he would be the one to decide the outcome. This was quite amazing to Jeff and me since a similar sentiment was previously expressed in Dad W.'s blessing last Monday night. Also, Jeff and I have both felt more comfortable praying that Jonathan will have the strength to make the right decision rather than to plead for his life.

Jeff and I asked Carolyn, our favorite nurse, some hard questions yesterday trying to figure out the three scenarios – death, a miracle and complete recovery, or permanent brain damage. The doctors said there is definite brain damage to the parts that regulate personality and intelligence. How extensive, they don't know yet. I won't mind raising Jonathan again, but that scenario just doesn't fit in with the blessings and feelings we've had.

Today is the first day back for Jeff at work. The two little ones are at the Knarr's, and I'm ready to camp out another day in the Trauma Unit.

CHAPTER 6

June 22; Tuesday
Dear Friends & Family:
Good news from today. His ICP is considerably down. If it continues to stay down, then they'll wean him off the barbiturates used in the drug-induced coma which should at least take him to this Sunday. An MRI could then be possible as well as using a tracheotomy instead of the ventilator. They did have to drill a new hole in his skull to get a better and more accurate ICP reading. My poor little boy.

Wonderful help continues to come from all around us. This allows me to be at the hospital most of the day. We made a tape of our Family Home Evening* for Jonathan with each of us recording our thoughts for him. We then took a "field trip" to the hospital. Although we're not quite ready for Lauren and Peter to see Jonathan, they did get a feel of what it's like at my "home away from home."

We continue to be amazed and uplifted by the day-to-day spiritual experience all of this is. The line is often thin between heaven and earth that helped Jonathan prepare for this and is helping him prepare for the decision he needs to make – that we are certain of. What a loving, caring, and personal Father in Heaven we have!

June 21, 1999; from our Family Home Evening tape to Jonathan:

My opening prayer: "Our dear Heavenly Father - We're thankful for the opportunity to have Family Home Evening tonight and recognize that we miss Jonathan, and yet know that he is in thy hands. We're thankful for this time of faith and strength and courage and trust in thee. We pray that it will also be a time of growth and understanding and strengthening of testimony. We pray for our Jonathan that he will be able to do the right thing, that he will have the strength to make the right decision, and that he will feel as little pain as possible, and that he is happy wherever he may be. We pray for thy Spirit to guide and direct our thoughts and actions. We ask a blessing to be with the hospital staff – the doctors and the nurses -- that they will use wisdom and be guided in what they decide to do with Jonathan. And we pray that we will enjoy this night and know what to say to help Jonathan get better. These things we say in the name of Jesus Christ, Amen."

Jeff: "If you were there with Jonathan, what would you like to say?"

Peter: "I miss you."

Jeff: "What else would you like to say?"

Peter: "I love you."

Lauren: "Our family's not the same without you, Jonathan.... I love you Jonathan. I'll be nice to you forever and ever."

Andrew: "There's been a lot on my mind. It's really been different without you.... You really don't know how much you love someone until they're not around. I love you very much, Jon."

Mom: "You've heard a lot from me and seen a lot of me... hopefully somehow, 'cause I'm there right by your bed. The routine is that I try and get there about 10:30, come home at 6:00, and then we have a nice supper break, get rejuvenated, and then go back at 9 for a couple of hours before we settle down for the night. I was just thinking today about how we are spending so much time together. I must have set a record of time I've spent with you without asking you to do something for me! I guess the only thing I want from you now is not to take out the garbages, to bring down your laundry, or pick up your shoes, or all that other stuff I would tell you to do. The only request I have is that hopefully you'll be able to come back to us. But I think it's more important not what I want but what you want and what you need to do.

It does comfort my heart to be there. I don't know how much good it's doing for you, but I'm glad I'm there. I want you to know that I'll do anything for you. And that I love you. Always have. You've always been very special to me. We all miss hearing your voice and look forward to that time when we'll hear it again."

Dad: "We miss you Jonathan. We look forward hopefully to seeing you back, but it depends on what you want and what Heavenly Father wants you to do. We've had some very special experiences and have a lot to ponder upon because of the situation. We hope that you will keep us in mind, and remember that your family does love you very much and that a lot of people love you. You're a very special guy."

CHAPTER 7

June 23; Wednesday morning. *A few of the thoughts running through my head.... What do the nurses and doctors really think when they see my son? Will his mental illness and chemical imbalance go away because of this injury? I told the Lord today that, even if Jon has to lose some of his intelligence, it would be worth it just to get rid of this dark plague. No matter what happens to his mind, though, his spirit is unchanging – from the premortal life* to the eternities, even during this glitch.*

June 24; Thursday morning.

Dear Friends and Family:

Today was a big day for Jonathan. In my eyes, it marked the day he went from acute life-and-death care to long-term care. He had successful surgery in the morning in which the doctor replaced his ventilator with a tracheotomy. This is better for his overall health, mouth, lungs, and vocal chords. The doctor also put in a permanent filter that will catch any blood clots before they reach his lungs. This takes away the possibility of sudden death. He could still pass away from complications such as pneumonia, but it was still a relief to our minds.

Today also marks the day they took him off all medication including the barbiturate, blood pressure, and ICP meds. They still give him morphine occasionally for the pain. It's when they take the ICP bolt out of his head and can wash his hair for the first time that I – his mother – will be rejoicing! Hopefully at that point they will also be able to do an MRI. We're guessing that may be on Monday.

The oral surgeon came in yesterday and checked out his fractured jaw. He said it is healing nicely without him having to do anything. Yay! That takes care of all his broken bones. The cuts to his face are healing well. It's his left ear that may show permanent signs of what he went through. Not bad, though! We got the pictures back yesterday of the car. Unbelievable. The telephone pole made a direct hit to Jonathan's car door. How could he have survived such an impact? The doctors tell us that he went with inadequate oxygen for over an hour while they tried to get him out of the car. Their other concern, of course, is with the jarring on impact to the brain. He still shows no signs of coming out of his natural coma, but that shouldn't be until a few more days when the barbiturate is completely out of his system. He is back to reflexive movements which is still good to see. He also coughed a number of times yesterday which will help get rid of the pneumonia a lot quicker.

Jeff and I decided that we will fast* again on Sunday since next week is when we really need to start seeing signs (any signs!) of Jonathan coming out of his coma. If you so desire, please feel free to fast with us. We know prayer and fasting do help because we have directly felt the unusual calm and peace that has come through these heavenly pleas. We continue to try and keep our spiritual vessels open to the whisperings and comfort of the Spirit. How good that feels!

Again, thank you so much for your emails and other expressions of love and concern. I wish I could respond to all of you individually. Perhaps if this is a test of endurance, I will have that opportunity! I do want you to know just how touched we all are by this outpouring of love for Jonathan and our family. It feels incredibly good and warm.

June 24; Thursday morning. *What mixed emotions this morning! Right now I feel a sense of relief since the OR just said Jonathan will be back from surgery in 10 minutes. Shortly before that I had this feeling that if he was to die, it* would be during the surgery. Otherwise, we're probably looking at the only other possibility of death being taking him off life support. But then that would be our decision and not Jon's. As I thought of this, then I began to see that I wouldn't have had an opportunity to see Jonathan alive again.... But he made it through the surgery! Does that mean he'll make it? Has Jonathan decided yet what will happen?

During these past 10 days, there have been three families here in the trauma unit here for the long haul. 16-year-old Willie Petersheim was in a car accident four days before Jon's along with his less seriously injured twin. He, too, has been in a coma, but is responding. Then there's Mrs. Fackler who got really banged up from the arms on down in another car accident. Including Jonathan, these three patients and their families have all had tremendous support. And because we're all here most of the day, we've gotten support from one another. What sweet and spiritual families the Petersheims and Facklers are! The Petersheims are a large Mennonite family and Mr. Fackler is a retired Presbyterian minister. What a bonus this support has been. These people could have been abrasive, obnoxious, bitter, insensitive, and non-religious, but they have been just the opposite. It's also interesting to note that all three car accidents were along the same stretch of road on US 222 south.

June 27; Sunday afternoon. *There's a new family on the scene. But this one isn't handling it well at all. There are accusations, anger, selfishness, and no room for God. The step-daughter has been so appreciative toward Jeff just listening to her. At the moment that's the only support she's getting....*

As I think back on that night two weeks ago, how quickly, how suddenly life can change. Where will I be one week from now? Where will Jonathan be? How about one month? One year? Here's my guess and then I'll read back some day and see just how close I was.

One week from now we'll be over at the Intermediate ICU. Jon will still have his pneumonia and he'll still be on the ventilator. One month will find him off the vent, no pneumonia, eyes closed but regular movements from the body. One year... this one's harder. I'm going to be optimistic and say that he's preparing to leave for his mission as a tribute to the miracle year he just went through.

CHAPTER 8

The thing about a kite is that it lives up in between
The dirty brown of gravity and the misty blue of dream
The thing about a string is it connects you to the sky
And reminds you what it means to live...
and love... and dance... and die.

-FROM "THE BROKEN STRING" – A SONG WRITTEN
BY MARK KUNKEL, JONATHAN'S UNCLE

June 27; Sunday

Dear Mark:

I came into the hospital this morning and was greeted by some wonderful sights and sounds. Carolyn, the nurse, had put on your "Would You Like to Dance" tape you recorded and sent. She had also cleaned him up and couldn't wait to see the look on my face when I came in. The bed was propped up, the bolt was out of his head, the EEG machine was gone, and most importantly his hair was semi-combed and washed. He's improving... I should say he's moving along faster than I thought. He was even going to go in for his MRI today, but then the machine broke down just as they were prepping him. It looks like he'll be the first one on the schedule in the morning.

Anyway, I just wanted you to know that you're a major part of his life right now, thanks to your beautiful music. It was fun to have Carolyn listen to Jonathan's voice on "I Will." Oh, how glad I am that you had him sing that song! Do you have any more tapes of him singing? Oh, how I love to hear his voice.

Music has been a sweet comfort for me, and I have a feeling it will also be a part of Jon's healing.

With love,

Annette

June 28; Monday

Dear Friends and Family:

.... They did manage to finally get an MRI done on Jonathan. The consensus: Even more extensive shearing throughout the brain, particularly in the front "personality" part of his brain as well as deep and near the brain stem. Shearing is a breaking of brain tissue that damages the different functions. The brain cannot repair the damage other than reroute around the damaged area. That's usually why rehab takes a long time, i.e. learning to swallow, speak, regulate body functions, etc. The doctors feel that we have a long road ahead of us and that there is definitely damage to the brain. We were rather discouraged by this news, but reminded ourselves that we need to wait and see what the Lord's "prognosis" is as well, and that it overrides whatever the doctor's is. Fortunately, all the doctors we have talked to understand and accept this fact.

Today was a better day for Jonathan. The part of his brain that regulates body temperature isn't working, but they have him on a machine that helps regulate that. He was calmer today and thus able to progress in his movements. Both Jeff and I were once again lifted as we talked to others, especially after hearing the MRI results. Jeff was able to talk to a woman tonight that had gone through a similar experience six months ago. We're always interested in hearing of others' experiences....

June 28; Monday night. *What a day. It began this morning with a phone call at 7:19 from Dr. Good. We had asked him to call during his rounds and give us his interpretation of the MRI. It wasn't good. Extensive shearing throughout most of* *his brain. Injury to the brain stem. A very long road ahead. He may never come home. Definitely damage to the brain; just how much can't be said. This news left my hands cold and wet and my mind numb. But when I talked to Jeff on the phone a half hour later, I began to feel the pain and reality of the situation. It hurt and I cried. I then poured my heart out in prayer. It was easy to talk to my Father. I already don't remember much, but I do remember wanting to be comforted and asking Him to put His arms around me. When I closed, I remember feeling a great desire to talk to someone. Immediately the phone rang. It was Aunt Helen, Mom's sister. Hearing a voice so similar to my mom's and someone I admire was wonderful! No... more than wonderful. It was definitely an answer to my prayer, another witness that He loves me. I felt much better after Helen's listening ear, comforting words, and strengthening faith.*

Even though I told Jeff he needn't come home, he felt impressed to do so. How glad I was for his presence. It was just one of those days that we needed each other. While Jonathan's prognosis wasn't good, his progress certainly was. After almost 2 1/2 weeks, we saw him open his eyes! (But don't get your hopes up. Unlike what we see in the movies, this is only one of many steps towards waking up from a coma.)

June 30; Wednesday afternoon. *Mom and Dad came Monday afternoon. Oh, their hugs felt good! It was difficult for them to see Jon, especially Mom. But I am so glad they're here for him... and me.*

Before we all went in, we watched a video on comas that my sister, Diane, had taped and sent. It was very informative and gave a stark picture of the worst case scenario. Yet as I watched this, I just got the impression that this wasn't what was going to happen with Jon. At this point, I knew that he had made the decision to stay here. Why would he choose to leave heaven behind for a life in which he would be in a coma or so debilitated that he couldn't be a part of our life?

In contrast, yesterday I read an article from the July 1999 New Era* ("He Was a Stranger") about a 16-year-old boy from St. George, Utah who was in a coma for five months and didn't go home until a year after his car accident. It talked about all the people, particularly the youth, that had been touched through his two-year recovery. Now, that's more of what I see down the road for us! I'm now beginning to see just how much our lives will change.

July 1; Thursday

Dear Friends and Family:

It's getting rather difficult to distinguish one day from the next and to remember when things occurred. I'm not complaining, though. I am so grateful that my life's merry-go-round has stopped so that I can focus on the one "horse" that needs fixing. My other "horses" have been whisked off to our Montgomery Family Reunion in Nauvoo, Illinois thanks to my parents who came up for a visit and will take care of them for me until their return Tuesday night. It is so nice to be able to focus completely on Jonathan. I shouldn't say completely since there is still a need to clear the head and forget about the hospital for a little bit. I was able to do that last night when I went back to playing in my weekly city league volleyball game. Jeff and I have found that balance is still an important key, even in this new schedule of ours.

Despite the gloomy MRI report, Jonathan continues to progress one baby step at a time. Something must be working in his brain stem, for he is now able to breathe on his own for up to eight hours a day! It will probably take him a few weeks to completely wean him off of the ventilator. Yesterday was the first day he didn't need the cooling blanket and machine to regulate his body temperature. This was a pleasant surprise, for that was another part of his brain that appeared damaged. He still struggles to try and move his body. We have noticed recently, however, that he tries to talk back to us by moving his mouth in a Clint Eastwood sneer, moving his arms a little, and even opening his eyes at times.

He's able to squeeze a hand a little, but not yet on command. Oh, if only he could talk! I have a feeling he has just as wonderful of things to tell us as we have to tell him. I truly feel that he, too, has been receiving comfort, love, and guidance, especially in his decision to stay with us.

Know that we continue to be doing well through this. We have certainly drawn closer to Jonathan. (He's probably sick of being with his mom so much!) Jeff and I continue to remain very close and connected, and our relationship and communication with our Father in Heaven has certainly been strengthened. We are also truly appreciating the part of our Savior's atonement* in which he suffered for our sorrows and grief as well. Do continue your prayers on our behalf. There is such power in prayer!

CHAPTER 9

July 3; Saturday night. *A few written snapshots of Jonathan's 19ᵗʰ birthday yesterday:*

- *Coming in to see him in the morning, and just breaking down in sobs. It hurt so badly to think of my son celebrating his birthday in a coma in the hospital. I wasn't angry; just sad and frustrated. Of all the times for Jonathan not to greet me with his facial smirk and arm movements.*

- *Carolyn the Nurse's gift to Jon was a real matching pair of hospital pj's complete with bottoms! No easy task considering the rectal thermometer, oxygen reading tube, catheter, and possible bowel movements. She had found a place to display his two paintings, rearranged the room for the expected company, and washed him up. How sweet!*

- *My gift to Jon was inviting all his friends to come and visit him during the day. I also bought him mylar balloons, a cake for his guests, and made a "Happy Birthday" banner.*

That evening Jeff, Melissa, and I headed over to the hospital's "employee only" parking garage roof with Michael the chaplain to watch the Fourth of July fireworks. He shared with us a conversation he overheard between two nurses the night of the accident. They were talking about "the boy just brought in" and how sure they were that he wasn't going to pull through. I guess we've already seen one miracle and look forward to many more.

July 4; Sunday evening. *This morning's church was a wonderful spiritual feast. Both Jeff and I were able to bear our testimonies.* The Spirit quietly helped me to say all that was in my heart. Jeff's was so touching. He shared some of the spiritual aspects of these past three weeks. It was very tender and insightful. Again, I felt such gratitude for the perfect husband for me and this situation. He's been such a strength and spiritual beacon.*

So let's try this again. Where will Jon be one week from now? My guess is that the pneumonia will be gone. So will the oxygen tube. He'll be sleeping less and awake more. And he'll still be here in Bed #6. I doubt there will be much change with his coma. We will have decided that Mechanicsburg will be his rehab, and we'll be preparing to move him there. Stay tuned....

July 6; Tuesday afternoon. *It's been a peaceful, pleasant day spent with Jonathan. At last! Quiet time with just him. I find that I like to spend this time with him moving his legs* and arms, singing to him, talking a bit, or just listening to music with him.

Jonathan has added two new reflexes. He is beginning to swallow again. And he yawns! Funny how we take these things for granted. I love to see him yawn; it's so human.

He's doing fine without the breathing and temperature machines. As soon as he gets clear of pneumonia, we can move him to rehab. Which one? That's the big question. Hopefully we'll know by the end of the week.

July 8; Thursday evening. Mom and Dad left this morning for Tennessee. Yes, I cried. In many ways, they have been my emotional life line as well as great helpers at home. I'm so glad they came up! I'm so glad they all did the family reunion, even though they said it wasn't quite the same without us.

CHAPTER 10

July 10; Saturday
Dear Betty –
   It's my goal to type a quick note to one individual whenever I pull up email. It's your turn.... I hope the rest of yours and your son's road trip was a success full of never-to-be-forgotten memories. It brings to mind the time Jonathan and I went out to dinner at his favorite restaurant, the Taj Mahal, a week before the accident. I wanted to thank him for sitting patiently for three hours at a talent show practice with me. He had reluctantly agreed to play for me if they wanted me to sing "Angel." It is now one of my choicest memories as I look back and remember the wonderful food and conversation we had together. I look forward to going back there with him again some day.

July 12; Monday noon. *Well, last week's predictions were all wrong. That goes to show just how unpredictable a coma can* *be. We are now over at Bed #17 in the IICU (Intermediate Intensive Care Unit). Jon's pneumonia level has been stuck at about the same level no matter what the doctors do. This means he can't move to rehab, and I doubt his coma level will change much until he no longer has to fight the pneumonia. He's back using the ventilator, only to try and push deeper breaths throughout his lungs.*

July 12; Monday

Dear Friends and Family:

I knew this evening that I would have an opportunity tonight to write this update, but I wondered if I should since it's been kind of a down day for me. But Mom and Dad called and reminded me that this is as much a part of Jon's recovery as are the "up" days.

....We're still not sure where he's going for rehab. We do know that, because he's at a 2 on the Ranchos scale, he'll have to go into subacute level (less than three hours therapy per day). I'll find out tomorrow if the hospital's rehab is the only one that will take him.

A bit about this Ranchos scale. It is a scale that indicates the different levels of coming out of a coma – 1 being comatose with no movement and 8 being able to function in the outside world. At about a 4-5 is when we might say that he's come out of his coma. The greatest gains are done usually in the 2-6 month time frame after the coma begins, but improvement can be done up to 24 months. And to think that just a month ago, I didn't know any of this stuff!

On to the not-so-good news. Today, it seemed such a struggle physically for Jonathan. His brain is still having a bit of a time regulating his temperature so that he always has a low grade fever. Yesterday, he started to perspire a lot – also attributed to his brain injury. And this morning, it seemed that he would start to nod off when his eyes would open wide, followed by his heart rate soaring to about 150, and then he'd set off the vent alarm indicating he wasn't breathing properly, followed by a coughing spell. He would finally settle down, and this would happen all over again. It was draining on him as well as his mother. All I could do is wipe his brow with a cold washcloth and speak soothing words to him. Can you tell my heart is aching? For some odd reason, I was able to handle it better emotionally when it was the life and death situation. Now, I just feel so helpless.

I know that many prayers are going out on Jon's behalf. There is power in prayer. There is power in the priesthood. There is power in faith. There is power through Jesus Christ. How can we not but hope? And trust.

July 13; Tuesday morning. *Today is the one month anniversary of the accident. I'm writing this with hospital gloves and gown on here in Jonathan's room. I came in this morning to find that the pneumonia is gone, but apparently he now has MRSA – a highly contagious, antibiotic-resistant infection. They check weekly to see if it is cleared. Two clearances and we can get rid of the isolation level precautions. In other words, it's going to be awhile until I can touch my son. That part hurts. Fortunately, they don't have to wait for it to clear to send him to rehab.*

Which brings up my other frustration. The insurance company wants to wait until he's at about a level 4 for him to move to rehab. But I feel he can't progress as well until he's in rehab. So in just one week's time, we've gone from looking at rehabs for acute level, to the hospital's rehab for sub-acute level, to its ICC unit (a skilled nursing facility). The worst possible scenario – a nursing home – is just one notch down from that. Despite Jon making tiny little steps each day, it may not be enough. But who am I to say? This may be one of those times that the Lord's time table is not mine.

July 13; Tuesday

Dear Kenny and Denise –

What a sweet gesture! Thank you so very much for the beautiful dove ornament. When we hang it on our Christmas tree this year.... Well, I hope Jonathan will be able to do that small but significant act. Regardless, we'll always remember this bittersweet time that we're all going through right now.

Please feel free to come and visit any time. Our schedules have been kept fairly simple these days, and certainly flexible for visitors. If that's not possible, then feel free to write a letter to Jonathan that we can read to him. Or have your family make a tape that we can play for him. I truly feel that he can hear and recognize voices that can bring him comfort during this anxious time. What to say? Share memories that you have of Jonathan. Share your doings, thoughts, and feelings. Whatever comes to mind!

July 19; Monday

Dear Friends and Family:

Yesterday was a banner day for Jonathan! So many bits of good news all in one day. It began with a 7:30 a.m. phone call from Cathy (the social worker) at the hospital letting us know that our insurance company approved Jon to be moved to the hospital's rehab unit, using the 180 days of "skilled nursing facility" as opposed to the 60 days rehab allowed. That was perfect! This, of course, continues as long as he is progressing. *[Author's Note: Looking back, Jonathan was exactly where he needed to be every step of the way. The 60 days of paid rehab needed to wait until he woke up. Even having the accident as an "adult" at age 18 made a huge difference. Because of this perfect timing, our medical bills were kept to a minimum.]* When Jonathan moves up to a level 4, then we will probably move him to Mechanicsburg Rehab.

And speaking of levels, that's something else that happened yesterday. He moved up to a level 3 on the Ranchos scale! When we met for an hour with the doctors and therapists that afternoon, they gave us that bit of news. Apparently, the speech pathologist noticed that he was looking up and down and all around when she put one of his paintings in front of him. He was also able to focus his eyes on her. In addition, the occupational therapist noticed that he – often enough to be documented – followed her commands to squeeze her hand and move his leg. Yay! I have a feeling it will be a long time until he gets to level 4 (physically and verbally thrashing around in confusion), but we'll simply continue to be patient. (And yes, that's apparently a good thing!)

Other news from the meeting.... Jon's MRSA was a false alarm, due to him having the less worrisome negative version. Phew! He had his first x-ray that showed the pneumonia to be virtually cleared up. Rehab has ordered a wheelchair fit to Jonathan's size and needs so that he and his brothers can do wheelies in the hallways. *And* he was moved to rehab! That means no more monitors and no more IV line. He still has the trach, catheter, and stomach feeding tube. When I went in to see him today, his eyes were wide open and his arms were moving about. His muscles are still very tense, but he seems to relax when he gets visitors. I'll come in periodically during the morning therapy hours to observe so that I can do some of the things taught later in the day. Otherwise, I'll more than likely just spend afternoons with him and Jeff will continue to go in the evenings.

As I look back on this very up and down week, I'm beginning to understand how things will be in the months (years?) to come. By the end of the week the clouds of discouragement were blown away by the rays of hope and light. Faith is strengthened, patiently waiting for the next test.

CHAPTER 11

Why should we mourn or think our lot is hard?
'Tis not so; all is right.
Why should we think to earn a great reward
If we now shun the fight?
Gird up your loins; fresh courage take.
Our God will never us forsake;
And soon we'll have this tale to tell –
All is well! All is well!

– "COME, COME, YE SAINTS" HYMN #30;
WORDS BY WILLIAM CLAYTON

July 23; Saturday
     Dear Friends & Family:
     First off, for any of you who can go in and visit Jonathan, don't be too alarmed when you see him in arm

and leg casts. The therapists are doing what's called serial casting to keep his arms and legs ready for when they can get back to normal use. Because his muscles are so rigid, they no longer straighten completely out, so hopefully this will help.

While there, check out his new wheelchair just right for his needs. Since his brain still doesn't tell his body muscles to work, this chair keeps him secure, especially his head. We're not quite ready for wheelies down the hall, however, since he's still lugging around his food and oxygen stand.

Another new thing you can add to the list of permanent fixtures in his "bionic" body is a shunt that will be placed underneath the skin in his scalp on Tuesday. This morning, Jeff and I talked to Dr. Good (whom I affectionately refer to as "Dr. Doom") about the changes noticed in a recent MRI done. According to the pictures, Jonathan either has atrophy and/or hydrocephalus. Atrophy is a wasting away of brain cells. Hydrocephalus is fluid on the brain that isn't properly being drained. There's nothing one can do about atrophy, so we're hoping that it's the hydro one. Dr. Good did say that he definitely has some atrophy caused from the lack of proper oxygen that first hour after the accident, but hopefully it's not really extensive. Remember reading about the girl who just had half of her brain removed and she was still able to walk and talk? I could probably also think of a few of us that only use "half a brain!"

(**From my journal:** *"How did I react to this latest bit of news? It was just a bit painful seeing pictures of my son's brain with so many empty spaces. Later the thought occurred to me that if he had been at Mechanicsburg like we originally anticipated, this problem would have gone undetected since they don't do CT scans or MRI's. That to me was another needed sign that Jon is where he should be and that the Lord is still very much involved in this plan of recovery."*)

One of our family's favorite Family Home Evening activities is to play hide-and-go-seek in the dark in the house. The other day I got thinking how much fun it would be to play it one Monday night right there at the hospital! Of course, we couldn't do it with the lights out, but still.... Imagine all the neat hiding places! Our faces are so familiar by now that probably no one would suspect a thing. What fun! Do you think the family would go for it? Andrew: "No way. I'm sure there are rules against playing hide-and-go-seek in the hospital." Lauren: "Somebody has to go with me. Otherwise, I'd be too scared." Peter: "Sure, let's go!" Jeff: "Are you feeling okay, dear?"

Until next time,
Annette

P.S. For those of you who can visit, the new visiting hours are 4-8:30. Feel free to talk in simple terms to him, sing to him, or just sit with him. You might even see if he'll focus his eyes on you. Or do a hand squeeze or thumbs up command. If his eyes are half closed, feel free to work with him. Let him sleep only if they're fully shut. Anything is much appreciated!

July 27; Tuesday noon. *They just wheeled Jonathan off to surgery to have his head shunt put in as well as his trach replaced. It was odd. My escort commented on how lucky Jonathan was to have me. The anesthesiologist didn't think I was his mother but someone who worked here. Jeff and I continue to have people telling us how amazed they are by our optimism, our faith, and our good natures. This perplexes me! When you <u>know</u> that the Lord is in charge and this is all part of <u>His</u> plan, why despair? Why worry? Yes, there are the occasional days, but for the most part, days go by of waiting and wondering. And in between, there are bright spots of light and warmth, like last night when Jeff and I ate dinner and visited with Bob and Cathy Breuninger. Or sitting outside the hospital enjoying the sunshine and fresh air while eating a bagel and drinking a Snapple smoothie.*

July 28; Wednesday

Dear Family:

I feel like I'm ready now to share a letter that Jonathan wrote to his dear friend Melissa some time in May of this year:

"I'm not sure I can stay here long. Something creeps up on me like an approaching waterfall on a river. It's like somehow I'm being warned of some drastic turn my life is about to take. Perhaps not drastic... just change. This much I know – there is a task I must serve. I cannot imagine how I would; I feel totally unprepared and inadequate. This is why I feel some change would be drastic....

Everything I do seems suddenly, strangely significant, as if someone was watching closely. I find immense symbolism in everything I do or create. Nothing seems coincidental.... Pulls are very extreme, as in I feel very strongly I should stay and also very strongly I should leave.

You know, looking and reading back over this, it all seems very stupid, and I shouldn't give it a second thought. But my name is being called over and over again. I know it is being called by something or someone much more powerful than me. I know something is going to happen very soon.... When we are told something will happen soon... we are given a knowledge of its existence, and a warning to prepare."

When I first read this letter on June 24, even then I didn't fully understand this "waterfall" that he would experience. In fact, I still don't. But I do know that this journey down that "river" is not self-guided, but rather guided by Someone who knows every turn, every dangerous rapid, and most important, the best course to take. I suppose that's why it's fairly easy to let Him do the steering. In the meantime, we hang on through the rough spots but also take time to enjoy the passing scenery.

July 30; Friday afternoon. *I just finished cutting Jonathan's hair. Not my best hair cut but it'll due for now. They shaved quite a bit of the back off for the shunt, so I had to be somewhat creative. I had the strong impression that Jon did not want it all shaved off like they often do in these cases. I also didn't want him looking like a prisoner in a concentration camp, so I kept "the redheaded mop" on top. After I finished, I wondered just how many more times I'd be cutting his hair in a rehab setting. Will he be able to hold his head up next time? Will he require any other funky hair cuts? When will we be back home?*

July 31; Saturday morning. *As I was walking out of the hospital yesterday to go home and get my cutting supplies, I began humming as I often do. When I realized the song was "Come, Come Ye Saints," I began to quietly sing the words. When I got to the part, "All is well. All is well," a warm, powerful whisper of the Spirit went through me and I knew that my Father was sending a message to me. With Jonathan not improving immediately like we had anticipated, I'm finding I need that reassurance that "all is well." Even I'm beginning to wonder, "How am I able to hang on?" Only through a complete trust in God with His plan and His time table.*

Jeff was also feeling kind of down that morning, and in his prayer he prayed that I would have a direct message from the Spirit, for he often gets lifted by my being lifted. I remember him asking me that evening if anything unusual happened that day. I shared with him what little news there was about Jonathan. He asked again, and as an afterthought I said, "Oh yeah, on my way out of the hospital..." and I shared the feelings I had.

No matter how many times the Lord shows His hand in our lives, I will always be amazed at His personal touch as well as love for each one of us. And hey, prayer works!

August 1; Sunday

Dear Friends & Family:

After a rather hectic Sunday, I need a few minutes to chill and unwind before I pack for Girls Camp*. Yep, I'm going, but just for two days. I'll be back for another two days, then Peter and I will be flying to Georgia for four days to spend with my family – many of them performing in their stake's musical, "Goin' to Zion." It's going to be a little tough leaving Jonathan, but I've lined up "substitute moms" to be with him while I'm gone. I've also given Jonathan explicit instructions that he needn't wait for me to come back before he makes his next move. ("Feel free to get up and get yourself a bowl of ice cream while I'm gone, Jonathan.") Speaking of these sub moms, I was so impressed by the many willing to sign up when I went in to Relief Society and told them what I needed. Such a wonderful, thoughtful, selfless group of friends we have!

Okay, now about Jonathan. The shunt is in place and working fine. Unfortunately, the ordeal set him back physically. He developed a high temperature and heart rate. It appears it's dehydration. Solved that problem. Had some really bad sweats that left him pretty wiped out. His face got swollen from the shunt, but that has almost gone down. Yet today when I went in, he was back to high temperatures, spiking at over 102. After the doctors consulted with each other, they narrowed everything out but possible blood clots. In order to check that with an ultrasound, they needed to take off his leg casts which they did this afternoon. We don't have the results back yet, so we continue to wait and wonder. In the meantime, Jonathan just doesn't feel up to working on getting out of the coma. I spend my time with him mobilizing his arms and legs. One good piece of news from today was that he had less tone and more flexibility than I've seen in a long time. Oh yes, and the day after his surgery, he kept lifting his head up off the pillow which he had not done before. It's the little things.... We keep waiting and wondering, praying and hoping.

CHAPTER 12

When you walk through a storm
Hold your head up high
And don't be afraid of the dark

– "YOU'LL NEVER WALK ALONE"
WORDS BY OSCAR HAMMERSTEIN II

August 7; Saturday
Dear Friends & Family:
I'm here in Alabama with Peter visiting my sister. The Montgomerys are all converging in Georgia for the church musical my brothers and their families are participating in. It's so good to be with my family!

I left Jonathan in better shape than when I went off to Girls Camp. By Tuesday, Jonathan's fever was gone. They think it may have been from that IV line they put in his chest that got infected, so they quickly removed it. By the time I returned on Wednesday, the puffiness in his face was gone as well as the profuse sweating. In other words, he was back on track physically with the focus once again being on the brain injury.

When I left him yesterday, he seemed much brighter and more able to focus for longer periods of time. That morning, I had him looking at his Picasso art book or following some of my simple commands for about a half hour – a new record! They mentioned in our family meeting yesterday that Jonathan may remember everything that happened prior to the accident, but probably can't remember from one day to the next. That must be why he never tires of looking at his three paintings, the kids' pictures, or the few art books we brought in.

Dinner is almost ready, so I better wrap this up. This has been a tough week for me emotionally, having left Jonathan for Girls Camp and then having most of my girls there getting the stomach flu. Yes, I had a few good cries followed by some very earnest prayers. I find I don't lose faith so much as I do trust, with that trust being replaced with worry. But then as I talk to my

Father in Heaven who knows all, that worry is once again replaced with trust and peace of mind. Thank goodness Jeff has had a fairly stable and up week. His faith, wisdom, and strength have been such a blessing in all of this.

We continue to see ourselves with a long road ahead of us. But as that road becomes more familiar, we're finding it's not such a bad road after all. Thanks for walking with us, thus making it more bearable

August 4; Wednesday evening. *I'm back at the hospital with Jonathan. His new trick is raising his head up off the pillow. It was good to see him again. Does he remember me or even know who I am? When I came in, his eyes were closed so I didn't disturb him. But when I began talking to someone else, he did open them. He did the same thing when I turned on "The Simpsons!"*

I have a feeling that I will never forget this year's Girls Camp. Monday was such a good day. I remember commenting in the evening, "The weather is perfect. Kate Udall, my camp director, is fantastic. What then will be the refiner's fire that seems to happen at every Girls Camp?" Well.... Tuesday Kate mentioned at lunch time that she hoped she wasn't pregnant because she wasn't feeling too well. By supper time she had thrown up with diarrhea following shortly thereafter. She wasn't pregnant but she did have the dreaded and highly contagious stomach flu that is spreading around Lancaster County. She ended up going home that night. Then Heather Henne threw up and also went home later that night. After sending off the rest of the girls to bed, I sat down alone and cried trying to get it all out of my system. I was worried about Jonathan. I was worried about the Young Women. I was worried about myself. Then I prayed until that worry was transferred back over to trust. I soon drifted off to sleep. Sherma Woolstenhulme came to relieve me as planned this morning at 11:30. But I can't help wondering how many more girls will get sick by the time camp ends on Friday.

August 5; Thursday morning, 10:00 a.m. *I've hit another low point. I thought I got all my crying out at camp, but I need another good weeping session. Unfortunately, there isn't really a private place here at the hospital to do that. Buck up Annette! I awoke this morning with a headache and I'm feeling faint. Not sure if it's stress or the beginnings of the dreaded flu.*

Midnight. *I ended up having another crying/praying session right here in Jon's room. Kim, the caseworker, heard me crying and came in to see if she could help. At first I just wanted to be alone, but I soon found it was good to talk it over with her. I was then ready to talk it over with Heavenly Father. And I felt Him talking back.*

To finish the Girls Camp saga.... When I got home from the hospital last night, I got a call from Laura Knarr asking me to meet her halfway since now my own daughter and Kelly Jackson were sick. Then Ashley Miller got sick, so of course her sister and her best friend and her best friend's sister wanted to go home as well. As of today, that leaves only three girls remaining, and I have a feeling they're leaving early as well. When I heard all this I said, "Laura, do me a favor. When way down the road you see the blessings that come from this, please let me know." That's how discouraged I was!

August 7; Saturday

My Dear Young Women:

Greetings from Alabama where I'm staying with my sister. We'll be heading to Atlanta in just a little while to see "Goin' to Zion!" Despite being so far away from you, I've still thought about you a lot and especially what we went through at Girls Camp.

Remember the scripture in which Jesus Christ talks about how He feels like a mother hen who wants to gather her chicks close to her to comfort and protect? Well, that's about how I have felt this past week towards you all. At Girls Camp I wanted to protect you from the sickness. And now I want to comfort you. Don't you suppose that's how Heavenly Father must also feel? With all that I've recently gone through with my own sick Jonathan, I'm glad that He, in His great wisdom, has not protected me from all the growing that I have had to do to cope with this tragedy. Yes, I wish that He could have protected Jon from the natural consequences of that night. But rather, He chose to use this time to spiritually progress the Whitlocks and even their friends and family around them. I should say that he *gave* us the opportunity to spiritually progress. It has been up to each one of us whether or not we take hold of this opportunity.

Can you see that each one of you who was at Girls Camp has that same choice to accept or reject spiritual growth? Our choices will be shown through our thoughts, our words to each other, our attitude, and our personal prayers.

When all this happened to Jonathan, I had a definite number of choices. I could get angry. I could say, "Why did you do this, Lord?" I could withdraw from Him. *Or* I could trust. I could pray for strength. I could grow in my relationship with the Lord. I can honestly say I have chosen the latter and been much happier for it! Now, that's not to say I haven't had times where I've struggled or shed a few tears. But those times have always been followed with formal or informal prayers in which I talk to my Father about it. Together, we seem to be able to work it through.

You, too, have those same choices. And you'll probably have those same struggles. Yet when the right choices are made, you will be better for it, I promise you that.

Please feel free to talk it through with me. I've had a loving husband who never tires of helping me through my struggles. I want you to know that you have a loving Young Women President who never tires of helping you through your struggles. I love you all so very much! May God be with you all.

August 10; Tuesday afternoon. *Goin' to Georgia was great! It filled my spiritual and mental "buckets" – apparently to overflowing considering how many times I shed a few happy tears. I was a bit worried that Peter and I would get the flu, but no, we didn't (nor did Jonathan). I also began to wonder and pray if I was really supposed to go on this short trip, but yes, it was meant to be. I see it as a gift from a loving Father in Heaven who knows exactly what I need. Last week was my lowest point thus far. Goin' to Georgia to see "Goin' to Zion" and be with my family was just what I needed!*

August 11; Wednesday afternoon. *After a week of spiking temperatures, Jonathan is better physically, just not mentally. I haven't gotten him to follow any commands for a while. Father in Heaven, just exactly what is your time table? Just* *how long is long? We're coming up on two months here. I know all the hospital staff, even those that work on the other floors. People are starting to wonder where my work badge is. I wouldn't say I'm discouraged. It's just that progress is so slow....*

August 12; Thursday morning. *Shortly after I wrote my last entry, I met with Kim the Caseworker and Sue the Social Worker. Just prior to that, they allowed me for the first time to wheel Jonathan up and down the hallways without being hooked up to his oxygen. I suppose they were trying their best to ease the blow. We then reviewed the information from that day's staff meeting. Included in their report was having to prepare us for the possibility of moving Jon to a nursing home or bringing him home in case he doesn't show improvement with his brain injury in the next week or two. This would hopefully be temporary. But boy, what a psychological blow. I understood how difficult this was for Kim and Sue when they started getting teary. I held up pretty well until I came to talk to Jonathan about it. We'll fast again this Sunday and have Jeff give him a blessing. I told the Lord I would be content to just have a small miracle at this point, but I'm getting the feeling that we're going for the big one. "Trust in the Lord, [Annette], with all thine heart; and lean not unto thine own understanding." (Proverbs 3:5)*

August 13; Friday afternoon. *Two month anniversary of the accident. With the news of Jonathan probably going into a nursing home, Jeff and I have both shed many tears of sadness. Pure sadness.*

August 14; Saturday

Dear Friends & Family:

It's been a tough week emotionally for us. On Wednesday, I was told by the Rehab staff that Jonathan has one or two more weeks to show marked improvement or he will have to be moved to a nursing home. They hate to do this, but it's getting harder to justify him being there. We also got the results back yesterday of his post-shunt CT scan that showed no change. In other words, the large black area in his brain that we saw is probably atrophy and not hydrocephalus. That makes it tougher for Jon to find ways to reconnect around the brain injuries – but not impossible.

Needless to say, this has been difficult to accept for Jeff and me. I told Father in Heaven that I would be content with the "smaller" miracle of healing. But after having read over one of Jonathan's priesthood blessings from February 1999, I see that many of the great and promised blessings can come easier through a bigger, different miracle. Oh, but what a test of endurance and faith for us! Yet we still sense that (1) Jonathan is a very special son of God with a powerful and distinct mission, and (2) this is all part of a great and unimaginable plan directed by an all-knowing God.

We feel a strong need, especially at this time, for guidance, comfort, and answers from on high. Jeff and I will be fasting tomorrow. If any of you are able to join us, it would be so appreciated. Please continue to include us in your prayers. We have received such strength from knowing that many are talking to Heavenly Father on our behalf. Again, thank you.

CHAPTER 13

On bended knees, with broken hearts,
We come before thee, Lord,
In secret and in open prayer--
Oh, wilt thou speak thy word?
Feed thou our souls, fill thou our hearts,
And bless our fast, we pray,
That we may feel thy presence here
And feast with thee today.

– "BLESS OUR FAST, WE PRAY" HYMN #138;
WORDS BY JOHN SEARS TANNER

August 17; Tuesday
   Dear Betty:

Thank you so much for your recent email.   I appreciate reading your thoughts, ideas, and words of comfort.

I, too, often wonder how we are getting through this. We've had our times of sadness, grieving, and wondering, but there have definitely been more times of spiritual growth, understanding, and peace of mind. There have been those times that a spiritual light bulb seems to go off in my head where I better understand a doctrine or principle.   There are times that I feel a strength beyond my own capacity. And there are times when I literally feel my Savior's love.   These are the things that help me get through this. And wonder in it. And rejoice in it! Oh, but I would give it all up if I could have my Jonathan back.   But perhaps not, for I know if we asked God to cut His plan short, we would deprive Jonathan, ourselves, and who knows how many others a better chance to "bring to pass [one's] immortality and eternal life." (Moses 1:39*)

So in the meantime, I strive for that balance between faith and understanding.   Where may not yet understand, I need to exercise my faith while continuing my search for greater knowledge. For I know that God lives, and that certainly helps! And I know that He loves Jonathan (and all of us for that matter) beyond what we're capable of understanding with the fraction of the brain we do use!

Don't you just look forward to the life after this when it will be one eternal sigh of, "Oh, I get it now!"? Again, there are times when I ache to "get it now," but know that for reasons not yet completely understood, my perfectly loving Father in Heaven chooses not to divulge all at this time. And that's where trust comes into play. How often I have had trust be my solace these past two months. It is what drives despair and hopelessness away – two feelings that do no good.

Well Betty, this was just going to be a quick note, but I've found it to be very therapeutic to put these thoughts down on paper. But it is time for bed. Till later....

My love,

Annette

August 19; Thursday

Dear Friends & Family:

Thank you so much for your recent prayers and fasting. The immediate results were: (1) an inspired priesthood blessing, (2) a restored sense of calm and peace of mind, and (3) continuing to be led by the Architect of this plan.

(1) Jeff's parents and Melissa joined with us on Sunday afternoon as Jeff gave Jonathan a blessing that

reminded Jonathan of his responsibility in getting better and reassured us that he would recover, but that it would take time. It was so good to hear words of comfort and wisdom from One on high.

(2) Since Sunday evening, I have felt at peace again. It still saddens me when I think of what lies ahead, but I'm okay with it. Jonathan didn't make enough progress to warrant staying at the rehab, but a surprising blessing has bought us some time. Out of the seven possible nursing homes that our insurance works with, all either have no beds available or a few just don't take coma patients. So there's nothing we can do but keep Jon at the rehab until a bed becomes available. This will give Jonathan a few more weeks to improve. Perhaps he can even have his serial casting done by then.

(3)Perhaps the Lord is already leading us to another, even better place. I would not have thought that possible a week ago, but today I had the opportunity to talk to someone from Masonic Homes who came to evaluate Jonathan. Out of the seven nursing homes, they were the only ones truly desiring a coma patient. Needless to say, Jeff and I will take a tour as soon as possible. The uncertain part is just how long we'll have to wait for a bed. The rep said it would be at least two weeks. I hope our insurance company will be patient.

I finally got on the internet last night to read of others' experiences. I learned a little bit more, but I was somewhat disheartened by their situations. It seemed that at least one of three things was missing:

- good support system from friends and family
- an enlightened hospital/rehab staff
- trust in God

We continue to be hopeful yet realistic enough to prepare ourselves for the long haul. Again, I can't say enough about how important it is to feel the presence of the Lord in our lives. What a blessing!

CHAPTER 14

Be still my soul: The Lord is on thy side;
With patience bear thy cross of grief or pain.
Leave to thy God to order and provide;
In ev'ry change he faithful will remain.
Be still, my soul: Thy best, thy heav'nly Friend
Thru thorny ways leads to a joyful end.

—"BE STILL, MY SOUL" HYMN #124;
WORDS BY KATHARINE VON SCHLEGEL

August 22; Sunday
Dear Erin:
Thanks so much for telling me about your friend in the coma for seven years. Can you share any more details with me? For instance, where was she during this time – at home or in a nursing home? How

much has she recovered? Any words of wisdom for those waiting?

August 26; Thursday

Dear Friends & Family:

I'm not feeling so overwhelmed tonight thanks to the Young Women coming in and cleaning the house for Mutual tonight. I was once again touched by their willingness to serve and to even enjoy it.

Jeff and I still struggle with balancing time between home and rehab. I suppose this will be our challenge for the next year or two. How grateful I am, though, that I felt prompted to simplify my life by not continuing college classes, teaching at the New School, taking on piano lessons... even before I knew any of this would happen. Most days we can handle the pressure and reality of it all. But, speaking for myself, I find I need a good cry about once a week. It's a good release, but more importantly, it brings me closer to God and/or to my husband. (They both have great shoulders to cry on!) I'm not sure why I'm writing all of this except that many of you have wondered, "How do you get through this?" A balance physically, emotionally, and spiritually is essential. I suppose that's why now is a perfect time to "pay up" on my Christmas gift to Jeff. We're spending the night at a suite hotel near the Washington

D.C. Temple* tomorrow night while the kids stay at Grandma and Grandpa W's a half-hour away. It will also feel *so* good to finally get to the temple – something I've been aching to do since all this happened.

Some very good news about Jonathan – He's now able to sit in his wheelchair and keep his head up all the time. He also did very well today on the tilt table with neck and torso control. They strapped him to this board and then positioned it so that he could be vertical for the first time since this whole thing happened. He really responds well to Jeremy, the physical therapist. Yesterday, he got Jon to lift his eyebrows and furrow them on command. We're hoping this will eventually lead to a yes/no communication using those bushy eyebrows of his. Jonathan has also done it a few times for Jeff and me. When we ask him to do something, you can really tell that he's trying. Oh, how tough it must be for him to understand but have such little control over his body.

In the staff meeting yesterday, Dr. Polin suggested that he stay in the rehab for another two weeks to monitor his medications and finish up the leg casting. Perhaps by then Masonic Homes will have a bed available. If Jon must move and a bed isn't available, then Manor Care in York wouldn't be a bad "holding place" for him. Lauren, Peter, and I checked it out this afternoon. Jeff and I have gone from "Ooh yuk, nursing home" to "Hmm, that's more people with fresh ideas to work with Jon!"

When we understand that God has all the perfect answers and the map to the Big Picture, it does help us to be more patient and trusting. I do know this. I stand in awe that He would use such imperfect souls to carry forth His work. But part of that work is shaping these imperfect souls into glorious, perfect beings. Watching His plan unfold is one of the highlights of this time in our lives.

August 30; Monday morning, 11:30 a.m. *Just got in and was told Jon is still downstairs having his legs re-casted. Ah good, I can catch up with my journal. It's difficult these days to find spare time to write here at the hospital. The three or four hours I'm here are usually spent stretching out his legs or arms, giving him simple commands (the current one being, "Raise your eyebrows, Jon"), or watching him in physical therapy.*

This past week I was eating lunch with Peter and Lauren, and Lauren mentioned something about how stressed she was. For some odd reason, that opened the floodgates to my emotions. I ended up excusing myself and going up to my room for another good cry. Once again, that led to a very honest and open communication with my Father in Heaven. I remember asking Him if heavenly angels were surrounding us – ministering and concerned – just as our earthly angels were. I could feel my Father's love, but I told Him how much I looked forward to the day that I could see Him....

They just brought Jonathan back minus one leg cast. Apparently they couldn't get that right one on since his leg is so active now. Looks like they'll give him a sedative later. This was the first time I saw his leg in weeks. It was so skinny. I just cried when I saw it.

September 6; Monday

Dear Friends & Family:

I've been anxiously awaiting some quiet time this weekend to write this update. I'm finding that I look forward to sharing not only the update, but a few of my thoughts with you as well. Actually, it's more than a desire. It's a need that I have – to share a little bit of our lives in the hope that someone else may benefit by better understanding how the Lord works in our lives to bless us, teach us, and strengthen us. I have felt the Spirit guide my thoughts, and I hope you feel that Spirit as well when you ponder our situation.

Quite by everyone's amazement, our insurance approved Jonathan's stay at the rehab until this Friday. This gives them more time to get his leg casts bi-valved so they can go on and off. It also gave them time to do one more scan to verify that his temperature fluctuations are from his brain injury and not some hidden infection. They also x-rayed his right arm to make sure nothing was broken since he shows such pain when bending at the elbow. (Those, too, were negative.) So physically, Jonathan is doing very well. He's handling his new trach well with them cuffing it most of the time to allow air to go to his vocal chords, mouth, and nose. I did hear his voice one day when he groaned a number of times. Wow, his voice! Unfortunately, like so many of his other feats, he hasn't done it for me since. He hasn't done well with the eyebrow movements lately. It's not consistent enough to get a yes/no communication going. He does continue to be brighter and more alert, however. That in itself is a real positive, for it shows that he hasn't plateaued; he just progresses very slowly!

Jeff and I were talking on the way home from the hospital tonight about how we will look back on all of this. Will there be some bad as well as good in our lives? I can honestly say that there has not been any "bad" yet. How strange that must sound to some! What about the pain that we feel? Invariably, our times of anguish are soon followed by times of intense prayer as well as feelings, answers, and comfort from God. Such good experiences! What about the time lost in Jonathan's life while he remains in the coma? We don't think of it as lost time, for we know that this will be a life changing experience for Jon as well as for us. And from the priesthood blessings he's been given, we know that it will be a positive experience. As long as we don't give in to despair, bitterness, or hate our journey will be full of light and goodness.

That's something else Jeff and I were discussing the other day. It's as if this 12-week journey has brought us to a cave. We now stand in the middle of that darkened cave. The light that we borrowed from others' coma experiences is behind us as Jonathan's mind remains in darkness. We're having to take a less traveled road. But as we do so, we leave markers (i.e. our journal entries, emails, conversations, etc.) for others who may follow to make it easier for them. We're finding that part of exercising faith may require walking in darkness until we catch that glimpse of light. How long will it take? We don't know that. All we've been given is, "Be still and know that I am God" (Doctrine & Covenants 101:16*). We feel our footsteps being guided with each decision, but sometimes it's still pretty scary. "Trust in the Lord with all thine heart, and lean not unto thine own understanding" (Proverbs 3:5). I often say this over and over, especially nights like tonight when I looked over at my very skinny 19-year-old son so helpless and so far away.

Trust drives worry away. Hope balances the here-and-now. Faith brings peace of mind, understanding, and gratitude for a loving Father and Son. May you too feel trust, hope, and faith as you travel this journey with us.

September 10, 1999; Friday afternoon. *Yesterday, a typical day in the life of a CPM (Coma Patient Mom): Woke up at 7:30. Got kids off to school. Read for a bit. Housework for a bit. Made phone calls. Over to the hospital. Smells got to me again. Found Jon with a very drippy nose confirming that yes, he has a cold. Cleaned out his nose. Filled out another nursing home application since they are now "accepting a few applications." Talked to Dr. Eshelman in his office about the bronchoscopy he would perform that afternoon to figure out why Jon was coughing up blood. (I like him; he always asks how I'm doing.) Worked on Jonathan's range of motion exercises for his arms and legs. (I actually had to get up on the bed to get enough strength to keep his legs straight.) Ate a small lunch. Left for home.*

Picked up the two paintings of Jon's that Peter took to school since the kids were curious about his art. (Earlier in the week when it was Peter's turn to answer the question, "What was your favorite thing to do this summer?' he replied, "Go see my brother in the hospital." A glimpse into the heart of this special little nine-year-old I have.) Spent time with Lauren. The rest of the afternoon is a blur other than it was non-stop between kids' needs, phone calls, vacuuming, dinner (thank goodness Lynn provided supper), Young Women's volleyball practice since I had to coach, song practice, more phone calls, and catching up with Jeff.

I am now in the sun room. I just couldn't handle it any more in his room while Maria suctioned the blood clots out of his trach. Judy [name has been changed] *actually has Jon today, but she's on her break. I had a feeling it was her since I haven't seen anyone in the 1 ½ hours I've been here, Jon's hair isn't washed, he's lying on a dirty pad, the splint tabs were put on wrong... you get the picture. I'm going to have to get the nerve up and talk to Kim about getting another nurse. There's plenty of other good, compassionate nurses.*

Boy, do I need a good cry. But there's no place to do it here, so I have to keep fighting the tears back.

September 13; Monday

Dear Friends & Family:

It's been three months as of today since the accident. In a way that's kind of sad, but in another way, it gives us a good reason to look back with limited hindsight on this road we were given to travel. I can honestly say that through it all, we have never been left alone. This has been such a blessing. I can't even imagine how Job got through it all or even our Savior when the Father had to momentarily leave His side when He was on the cross (Matthew 27:46). We have felt such a guiding hand in all of this. There is such strength in that. For example...

I now know why Jonathan and I felt the Spirit so strongly in the decision for him to go to Southern Virginia College. The artistic and musical skills and tastes he developed there have been such an important part in the recovery process. This is evident as you enter his room. You might very well hear his favorite classical composer, Chopin, or look around and see his latest paintings. Just this weekend, two of his friends from SVC, Carrie and Will, brought his artwork back from the commercial show the dean of the art program, Mrs. Crawford, got together for him at her gallery. They're large works, but I did bring in one of them since the staff was so anxious to see more of his work. I am so glad that, because of such personal attention in this 300 student body college, he got one very big chance to strengthen his talents in a very big way.... And not to mention the lasting and significant friendships he developed with teachers and students alike. I doubt this would have happened anywhere else.

Whoa. I just got a phone call from Sue the social worker confirming that yes, Jonathan is moving today in two hours to Manor Care Nursing Home in York. "Didn't your son, Andrew, relay the message to us last Friday?" Apparently not! At first, this was a little bit of a blow, but as I've sat here, I realize it's time for him to move on and see what another environment and set of therapists can do for him. York is 40 minutes away from our house and not exactly on the way home for Jeff, but that's okay. Masonic Homes may never take him because of too many internal requests. These are the only two that have the less intense subacute rehab facility. Manor Care doesn't have any other coma patients right now, but they have had a few in the past. I toured the facility and saw that they had all the equipment that LGH Rehab has. So much of it, though, depends on how Jonathan likes working with the therapists.

Jeff and I have seen significant progress in the past few days. At one point, Jeff got Jonathan to raise and lower his eyebrows on command a dozen times in a row! And yet I couldn't get him to do squat last night. It helps me to be patient, though, when I think of Jon's brain as a 2500-piece puzzle that he has to figure out how to put together – with his eyes closed. Most coma patients are only given the 500-piece kind. Last night we met Matt, a 20-year-old who was putting together his own 2500-piece puzzle last year right in Jonathan's room. It wasn't coincidence that he and his parents happened to drop by to say hi to the nurses last night, just when Jeff, Andrew, and I were visiting. Oddly enough, Marylou the nurse was just telling Jeff about Matt five minutes before they showed up, not having any clue that they were coming in. What a tremendous blessing it was for us to spend that hour talking with and observing Matt. I especially enjoyed asking his mom a million and one questions and getting such good answers. (Matt was found with a blow to his head in Boise, Idaho last August. Neither he nor his parents have any idea how he got to the side of the road with such a traumatic injury.) Matt didn't get to level 4 until three months from his accident. He had all the same complications as Jonathan, but is now walking, talking, thinking, and working. He still goes to therapy twice a week for another few months.

Just a quick update on what happened to Jonathan last week before I close. Thursday's bronchoscopy indicated some type of skin growth on his trach causing him to cough up all that blood. Friday they cauterized three polyps that had developed, probably because of irritation with the skin rubbing on the trach. His legs still aren't ready to be bi-valved, so I believe this morning they simply recasted him, trying for a greater range of motion.

I'll always look back on this past week as a very intense one, what with the blood and the cold he had and the major decisions to be made. But then again, I just might be thinking, "You thought it was intense then...ha!"

In just an hour and a half, they'll be whisking Jon off in an ambulance with me following in the Neon with all his stuff. I guess I better head over to the hospital and start packing!

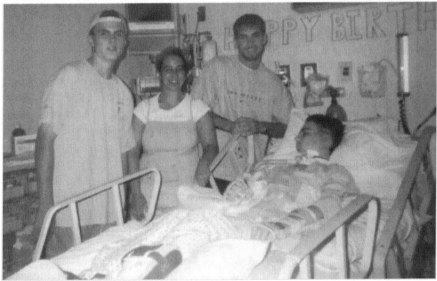

Bottom: Some of Jon's friends that came by for his birthday – Brad Boyd, Marissa Little, Zac Swavely.

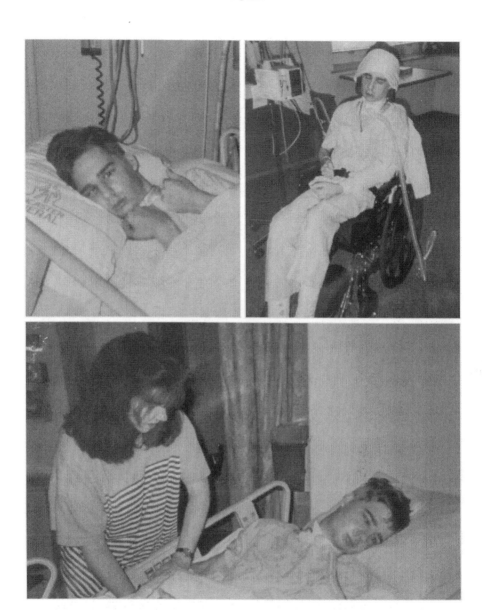

PART II

The Nursing Home

* * *

Sprinting has its season but it's not in the air today.
No, today's a day for plodding and for breathing deep,
they say.
It's the season of endurance and today is long and
bright,
Yes, the day will be filled with meaning enough for
many long dark nights,
In the long run.

Faith has its season and it's in my air today
Yes, today's a day for holding on to what seems so far
away
And when sorrow's all around you, I will stand right by
your side
We'll remember all the laughter and forget those tears
we cried
In the long run.

– "THE LONG RUN" 1ST STANZA BY MARK KUNKEL;
2ND STANZA BY ZACH BAILEY, JONATHAN'S FRIEND
AND FELLOW MUSICIAN

CHAPTER 15

If your world is filled with darkness, doubt and fear
Just hold on, hold on; the light will come

– "HOLD ON, THE LIGHT WILL COME" WORDS &
MUSIC BY MICHAEL MCLEAN

September 14; Tuesday afternoon. *I'm sitting in Jonathan's new room here at Manor Care Medbridge subacute rehabilitation center. Sounds okay, except that it's a wing off of Manor Care nursing home. So far it has the feel of a nursing home instead of a rehab unit. Yesterday had to be one of the toughest days for me yet.*

At 1:30, Jonathan was on the gurney and heading here in York in an ambulance while I followed in the Neon. I somehow beat the ambulance here. I was greeted by two patients smoking in their wheelchairs outside the entrance. I enter and go talk to the unfamiliar staff sitting behind the nurses' desk. They point me to his room. Jon soon enters, having slept the whole trip. The first nurse who comes in furiously writes notes here and there as she asks routine questions. I was amazed at how little she knew, but then I had to remind myself that they have only had one other coma patient. Lori, his case manager, soon came in and apologized for being so short staffed. Uh oh; not a good sign. It was downhill from there. Not only did they seem clueless what to do with him, but they hardly did anything with him. It soon became apparent that I would need to stay more than a few hours.

Fortunately, Lori allowed me to stay overnight in the empty bed next to him. When Jeff showed up about 7:00 last night, I was pretty frazzled emotionally. It was so hard to deal with leaving behind those that knew Jon's condition intimately, acclimating him and the staff to the new situation, and having to walk that fine line between advocate and tactfulness. It didn't take long for a pattern to follow: (1) Something needed to be done for Jon's care. (2) I would ask about it. (3) "Let me check on that." (4) Nothing. No reply. No follow-up. (5) I would then either take it in my own hands or let it slide. Classic example: His missing wheelchair which apparently got left behind.

The worst of these battles has been with his feeding tube schedule. I began to be concerned by yesterday evening when I knew he hadn't been fed food or water the whole time I was with him. After going the rounds with a number of people, I finally went to the nurses' desk at 11:00 pm. and said, "Look, I'm going to bed, but I can't until I know that Jonathan will get fed first." She finally admitted that they weren't planning to feed him until 5 am! Seventeen hours without food or water? Unacceptable! They were assuming that LGH fed him at 1:00 pm – which they hadn't – and the discharge orders had the night schedule written down incorrectly. I finally convinced her to feed him that night which they did. End of story? Nope! I again got concerned when they skipped his 9 am and 1 pm feeding. Lori finally admitted that they don't feed their peg tube patients during the day; just a drip at night. It took some more wrangling to get her to look into following LGH orders for the day feedings. Well, they never did, but I managed to get two of the nurses to give him water.

Our only hope is to talk to Dr. Davis who was supposed to make his rounds tonight. It is now 9:45 pm and we're still waiting for him to show up. My other battles – the catheter schedule, the splint/cast schedule (splint for his left hand, casts for his legs), bed rails – will have to wait.

Do you know what it feels like to be forced to put my trust in a new home and staff and find that they're doing a lousy job? Don't get me wrong. They're all good, sweet, and kind people. I guess they're just a bit overworked, understaffed, and sorely ignorant.

Jeff has been my angel husband through all of this. He has been my link to the outside world as well as my strength when he's here. He's had to work a short day today and probably tomorrow. So sweet. So loving. He even packed a dark Milky Way bar with my overnight stuff!

After way too many phone calls and some excellent detective work, my dear friend Laura Knarr finally figured out where I was and came to visit bearing granola bars, Excedrin, and two good shoulders to cry on. I poured out everything – my frustrations, my heartaches, my fears.

Another earthly angel came to my rescue, my mother-in-law. Without any hesitation, she came over today when Jeff called and will stay at home as long as we need her. I'm so worried about the children, but knowing she's there has calmed some of those fears.

So there you have it. I'll stay until I see that I can trust this facility to take care of my son's needs. This has been such a hard two days, but through it all, I don't feel abandoned. I still trust in Heavenly Father's plan. But rather than being a place where he could perhaps get better care in his coma therapy, I think that its purpose is to force new decisions and a new direction.

September 15; Wednesday afternoon. *It's been like night and day! Our first ray of hope actually came last night when we met Dr. Davis at 10:00 when he came to evaluate Jonathan. While checking him, he asked us questions, talked without being brusque, even asked us what our concerns were! He also had all the answers and none were, "Let me check on that." How refreshing! I'd say we all felt good about each other.*

When I got in this morning, the staff was bathing Jon, so I asked to see his chart. I was glad to read that they had taken his temperature, fed him, etc. I also noticed in Dr. Davis' notes that he's hoping to wean him off the trach in one to two weeks. Yay!

Today was his real first day of therapy. What a difference that made! Jon also sat in his old wheelchair for about three hours that had finally arrived. We spent much of that time watching home movies in one of the lounges.

I'm finding that the nurses and therapists are more laid back here. With therapy that is good. With nursing... well, we may just have to pick up the slack. Perhaps while Jeff and I teach them about Jonathan, they can teach us how to care for him. In the meantime, we continue to make friends with the staff. As Jeff puts it, that's a much better way to help Jon than going in this fighting.

I sang along with Michael McLean's "Hold On, the Light Will Come" this morning with great intensity and a few tears. I leave this evening with hope and a little more trust restored.

September 24; Friday afternoon. *There are so many things to write about, so many ups and downs... so little time. Jeff took a half day off today to observe and get a feel of what goes on during the day (and to give me a break), so I'm doing just that. I enjoy sitting out here at Manor Care on the bench amidst the trees. I choose the bench with its back to the nursing home so that I can escape for just a little while. Thank goodness for such beautiful days!*

This past week and a half here at the nursing home has been the hardest for me by far. I have cried just about every day – not for Jonathan but for myself. I have felt a need to be here as much as possible, but I still only make it in about 3-4 hours. Because I use all the time caring directly or indirectly for Jonathan, and take no time for myself, I come home physically and emotionally drained. It's to the point that I have difficulty thinking clearly. Should I clean the bathroom, go grocery shopping, or write an update? I honestly don't know, so I end up not doing any of it. That makes me feel even worse and gets me even further behind. Common phrases I've been telling myself: "It's so hard." "I don't know what to do." "Help me, but how?"

I'm hoping last night was my rock bottom in all of this. It helped to talk it out with Jeff. I also began to have flashes of inspiration make its way through the fog. I've got to find a way to turn this time around here from draining to energizing me. Yesterday I didn't know how. Today I can see it: Plan down time here (like now). Don't be afraid to play and sing for Jonathan and all the other residents in the "piano room." Read the scriptures to Jon. Sing the hymns for him. Ask friends and family to come here one day a week and be a substitute mom. (Oh, how I ache for my time at home.) Incorporate others in helping out; I'm still not sure how to do that one. Write a to-do list and stick to it. Push myself when getting things done at home and as a reward, spend down time with family. I'm sure as my head clears, more bits of inspiration will pass through and help me get out of this.

CHAPTER 16

When through the deep waters I call thee to go,
The rivers of sorrow shall not thee o'erflow,
For I will be with thee, thy troubles to bless,
And sanctify to thee thy deepest distress.

–"HOW FIRM A FOUNDATION" HYMN #85;
WORDS ATTRIBUTED TO ROBERT KEEN

September 27; **Monday**
Dear Friends & Family:
Wow. Where do I begin? This was *not* a good time to let two weeks go by between updates. So much has happened, but I suppose that's why I haven't been able to update....

The therapy here at Manor Care is much more laid back, and it was time for that. We've also appreciated their new opinions, skills, and outlooks. For instance, by the end of that first week, Jonathan was allowed to go for a few hours without being hooked up to a humidifier. This coincided with beautiful weather, so he got to enjoy the out-of-doors for the first time since the accident. Another decision quickly made was to bi-valve his leg casts a week after being transferred. That not only means more freedom for him, but after three months of sponge baths, he can now take a regular bath!

Two days ago, Dr. Davis took out the trach! All went well. We were anxious to see how he progressed now since sometimes coma patients really progress quickly when this obstruction is gone. Sure enough, when Jeff and Peter went in to visit yesterday they found a very agitated, perspiring, restless, and moaning Jonathan. How strange to hear his voice again, even if it was just deep, throaty moans. Was this the Level 4 agitation that we've been anxiously awaiting? When I mentioned it to the speech therapist this morning, she tended to agree with us that it was. By the end of the week, we should have a better idea. I went in to see Jonathan last night with Andrew. Even though I was prepared, it was still heart wrenching to see my son so uncomfortable. (One of the nurses tonight said that she had to change his bedding four times during the night he was perspiring so badly.)

Needless to say, I was anxious to see what he was like when I went in this morning. I found just the opposite! Jonathan slept most of the day, exhausted I'm sure from yesterday's ordeal *and* spiking a temperature of 103. All the usual tests have been ordered, so I'll let you know next time if the temp is from an infection or part of the ordeal he is now going through. When Jeff saw him tonight, he said he was once again awake and agitated although not perspiring quite as much.

So where do we go from here? If he continues to improve with consistent agitation and responses, then we'll move him to the Mechanicsburg acute rehab once we see a strong Level 4. If he tapers off and doesn't improve significantly, then we would take him home once our insurance feels he no longer needs a "skilled nursing facility." Hopefully there in a home environment he could continue improving with stimulation until ready for the rehab. We understand, however, that no matter how much we try to prepare for the future, it all depends on the day to day changes. Jon continues to plod along with his "2500-piece puzzle." One significant piece he recently put in was being able to communicate at times back to us with raised eyebrows for yes and closing eyes or scowling for no. I told you these therapists were good!

A side note. For the first time, Jonathan has a roommate. His name is Earl, he's 90 years old, and he loves "The Gospel Hour" on TV. Jonathan's a little shy and quiet, but other than that they get along pretty well. Let's hope they both have the same taste in music.

How are we doing? The kids have once again been real troopers in our new routine. I do try to make sure I'm home when they get home from school which helps. Unfortunately, that first two weeks found me with little left to give when I was at home. By the end of that second week, it was so bad that I couldn't think straight. Apparently you could even tell by looking at me that I was exhausted. By Thursday night, I knew what it felt like to be swallowed up in darkness wondering if there was any way to get out of it.

How did I get out of it? For one thing, I never felt that Heavenly Father was far from me. Also, sparks of inspiration began coming. I remember the first one being, "Annette, you've got to somehow turn this trip in to the nursing home from a draining experience to a bucket filling experience." At the time, I couldn't even see how I could not be drained, let alone filled. But the next day Jeff took off a half a day, giving me the chance to go outside with my journal and write – a very therapeutic thing for me. The next day Jon's college friends, Cara and Megan, came to visit. We found our way in to the piano room. I had already played a few times before but couldn't seem to get past the self-consciousness of performing for not only Jonathan but a handful of other residents. This time, however, I did get past that and actually enjoyed playing and singing my heart out (not to mention playing for the girls' beautiful rendition of "Angel"). Oh, that felt good! Other "bucket filling" experiences that weekend: laughing and having a grand ole' time at the Relief Society fall social with Jeff and our friends, attending the Relief Society annual broadcast, and taking a nap on Sunday afternoon. I now realize I must do *all* of President Ezra Taft Benson's* suggested twelve ways in which we can overcome sorrow, disappointment, and depression: 1. repentance, 2. prayer, 3. service, 4. work, 5. health, 6. reading, 7. priesthood blessing, 8. fasting, 9. friends, 10. music, 11. endurance, and 12. goals. *(From his October 1974 General Conference talk, "Do Not Despair.")* I'm also inclined to add one more: 13. laughter.

Regarding #9 on that list, I am still amazed and so very appreciative of all the little and big things that our friends do for us – from adding your names to the ward's* "Whitlock Service" sign-up sheets to the thoughtful gestures found in our mailbox. Your ever present love, thoughts, and prayers astound us. But more importantly, they sustain us.

October 2; Saturday morning. *It's been a much better week emotionally for me. It's also been a week of getting to know the staff and vice versa. They tend to hang out in here when they get some time. I find that interesting and positive!*

October 5; Tuesday

Dear Friends & Family:

When I just asked Jeff to describe this past week with Jonathan, his word was "progressive." "Be more specific," I said, hoping to edge him into writing this update. "Well, you can write about how he winks now at all the women that pass by." Hmm, maybe I better write this after all.

Yes, he can wink now! Isn't that weird? But no, he doesn't wink at all the women. However, he does like to wink at Lauren in particular. What we've noticed this past week is how he seems to want to communicate back to us. I think *he* even knows that his eyes are about the only thing he can control. Not all the time, but now and again the brainy "light bulb" clicks on and he responds rather well. After about five minutes, he clicks it off once again.

He has plenty to do, though, during the "off" times. We've moved his speakers right up to the head of the bed so he can listen to his classical, jazz, or church music. I'm subtly discovering the staff's talents, and so far I've gotten Eli to play his red violin (oh, and was that beautiful!), and Sonny to show off his puppets and bring in his dog. I don't know if it's his age or uniqueness, but they do love him there. When Jon's not listening to music and Earl's "Gospel Hour" is on the TV, he really checks out. You couldn't get him to respond at all when Earl had it on country music videos. Maybe Jonathan hasn't changed that much after all!

He also gets a good 1 1/2-2 hour workout in therapy each day. That's not counting the times Jeff or I will stretch his arms or legs. He still enjoys looking at art books and having your notes and letters read to him. We also wheel him outside on nice days. Or perhaps we'll take him into the piano room or the lounge for home videos. Hey, this routine doesn't sound so bad... unless you're in a coma.

We're getting an idea of what the future holds. His physical therapist mentioned yesterday that it could be another six months until he's ready for the Mechanicsburg rehab. If that's the timetable, then there's a good chance that he'll be coming home in between. We're looking at more comfortable and durable braces for his legs until he can walk again. We're maxing out the dosage of oral baclofen, the medicine he takes to try and ease the muscle tone. If we still don't get desired results, then we'll try a trial for the baclofen pump which can get great results but is inserted under the skin until he no longer needs it. In the meantime, Jeff and I continue to learn how to take care of him, i.e. change his diapers, wash his hair in bed, transport him, etc.

A spark of light in all of this – my mom is coming for two weeks! Admittedly, there are some days that I just want to take some of the weight off my shoulders. It will feel so good to be a daughter and not just Jon's mom.

October 10; Sunday (Excerpt from a letter written by Jeff to his sister)

Tricia:

I don't know if Annette told you about Jon's roommate, a 90-year-old man named Earl. Earl had Parkinson's and I had the opportunity to do small things for him on the evenings while I was there. I got to know him and his family to some extent. Earl's wife would show his visitors Jon's paintings and talk about him. One of the older ladies in particular would tell me that Jon was in her prayers.

Earl passed away last night at about 10:00, about 1 ½ hours after we left Jon for the evening. As I reflect on the meaning of all this – I don't believe in coincidences, and I don't think that Earl was there by chance – I am struck by what the Lord is telling me of death, of the resurrection, of our hope in Christ that Jon will be made whole at some point, whether in this life or in the life hereafter. Periodically the Lord sends people into our lives to remind us to not give up hope.

Thanks for your prayers and support. We love you dearly and hope that you feel the peace that we have felt through this.

Jeff

CHAPTER 17

October 14; Sunday
Dear Friends & Family:
Jonathan is communicating back to us! Jeff came home a few nights ago and told us that, without any prompting, Jonathan shook his head when asked a question! He did it again on command and for the occupational therapist that happened to be there. So the next day, I decide to give it a try. This time he nods his head yes. Today Sherma came in to read the children's book she wrote and Jon illustrated four years ago. She also brought in their first "fan mail" – a thank you note and pictures illustrated by a 2nd grade class that happened to get a copy of the book. I was pleasantly surprised to see how Jonathan seemed to be listening to every word and watching her every move. But I was even more surprised when he nodded his head when she asked him, "Do you like the drawings the kids did of the book?" That was nothing, though, compared to what he did tonight with his dad. Jeff asked him a series of

questions, such as, "Is it dark outside?" "Do you remember the hospital? The accident?" "Did Mom come in to visit you today?" – all with the correct responses. What a wonderful feeling to know that he can understand and respond back!

While Jonathan continues to entertain his guests with his talents at the nursing home, life goes on here at home. And rather nicely, I might add. Last Thursday I ended up having eight friends from church help me clean every imaginable nook and cranny while two more friends went to be with Jonathan. I even had dinner brought in that day. It still amazes me the outpouring of selfless love that so many are willing to give. That was also the day Jonathan slept the entire day. Apparently his body couldn't handle the increased dosage of baclofen, so we're going to have to "up" it a bit more gradually.

And now my mother is here for a few weeks! She, too, so willingly shares the burden, the cleaning, the cooking, the visiting, and the never-ending to-do list. Needless to say, I have shed fewer tears this week as I actually feel on top of things. I have also caught a glimpse of Zion where we "bear one another's burdens, that they may be light...." (See Mosiah 18:8 in the *Book of Mormon*.*) Truly there is great joy in service when coupled with Christ-like love.

October 22; Friday afternoon. *My time to write in this journal is so rare, especially now as Jon has gotten back his ability to communicate. He's made such wonderful progress these past few days.... It's just so difficult to leave him "alone...."*

October 24; Sunday

Dear Friends & Family:

...I'm finding the staff looking for excuses to come in and work with him to see if they can get him to answer their questions! It is so nice now to be able to sometimes know what he wants instead of guessing it. I say "sometimes" because he still has his light bulb off more than on and communicating only works well when it's on. He'll be out of this coma when the light bulb stays on+.

Have I mentioned that he is now eating a few things? It started with a Popsicle, then Italian Ice, and even some applesauce. Our goal is to have him eating pumpkin pie (minus the crust) for Thanksgiving. If you know Jonathan, then you know that's one of his favorite foods. He's able to eat now because he opens his mouth when asked to. That's the other improvement. He's getting back more control over his body. He holds his head and trunk more erect. He's even reached out and grabbed his toothbrush and paintbrush. Again, simple little things, but oh so important!

...We also continue to be blessed with helping hands and hearts. Mom leaves Wednesday. I've already scheduled a good cry from 2:00 to 2:30 between the time she leaves and the time one of my meetings begin. How am I going to do it without her? This has definitely been a two-woman job. But then again, I have been blessed with in-laws just two hours away, generous neighbors, faithful church friends... even strangers offering their kind words of comfort. It's just going to have to be a "many-people job!"

I am also touched to hear of the many prayers given on behalf of our son. How it must also touch our Father in Heaven's heart as well. Mom suggested that I tell of specific needs that can be said in these sweet prayers. Right now, our prayers are that Jon will continue to have the ability to communicate, and more often. Also that all will go well with getting the baclofen pump in place – granted it's the Lord's will.

Here's another idea of something you can do. We noticed that he really responds well to other people's voices, letters, and visits. Please feel free to send him whatever, either to our home address or the nursing home. Again, thank you so much for your prayers, love, and concern. It means so much to all of us.

+[Our idea of "being in a coma" changed considerably throughout the ordeal. Like most people, our previous knowledge was gleaned from highly inaccurate TV shows and movies. We learned, however, that it is a gradual awakening of the brain, rather than just "waking up" one day and all is well. For Jonathan, we felt his "awakening" was when he could finally speak, although progress continued through the next few years.]

October 25; Monday afternoon. ...Last week I visited with Dee, a mother who has been taking care of her daughter for 13 years at home. Muriel was in a car accident when she was 21, but damaged the brain stem and has been unable to progress much beyond where Jonathan is. I was amazed at the love and stamina and spiritual understanding of this great mother. For 11 of those 13 years, she has had to do it without her husband who passed away. Could that be Jonathan? Could I be as valiant, organized, and courageous as Dee?

After our meeting that day, I went and saw Jonathan, expecting to see a male version of Muriel. To my delight, he looked more alert, more "there" with higher responses. I got the distinct impression that he will make it out of this coma. It might take months, but he'll be back.

October 29; Friday afternoon. ...Jonathan continues to improve with his communication – more frequently and *longer periods of time.... We get the impression that his intellect and personality haven't been damaged permanently and that he understands more than expected at this stage.*

October 30; Saturday noon. *Surprisingly, I have rather enjoyed these trips back and forth this past week, thanks to a beautiful autumn....*

* * *

Heavenly Father, are you really there?
And do you hear and answer ev'ry child's prayer?
Some say that heaven is far away,
But I feel it close around me as I pray.

Heavenly Father, I remember now
Something that Jesus told disciples long ago:
"Suffer the children to come to me."
Father, in prayer I'm coming now to thee.

– "A CHILD'S PRAYER"
WORDS & MUSIC BY JANICE KAPP PERRY

October 31; Sunday afternoon. *I have some of my best talks with Heavenly Father in the car on the way up and back. This past week, as I tried to envision Jon's future, I mentioned to the Lord that, since his left side isn't working, it was okay if he couldn't walk or even play the piano or guitar again. But please, Father, let him paint again. This would be a way for him to give to others, even to influence others. It could also be his livelihood – even in a wheelchair. It was a mother's pleading request, and yet I still ended my prayer, "Thy will be done." And yet something inside me whispered that yes, he will paint again.*

Then today for the children's Sacrament Meeting presentation, the Primary* children sang their favorite song, "A Child's Prayer." It was so beautiful and touching – not only because they sang from the heart, but because of the whisperings of the Spirit. As I listened, I thought of how many of these same children had and are including Jonathan in their spoken prayers. There is great power in a child's prayer. The Lord listens and considers their words and their faith. He will not let them down. Jonathan will heal and the children will see this miracle and know that their prayers were heard and answered.

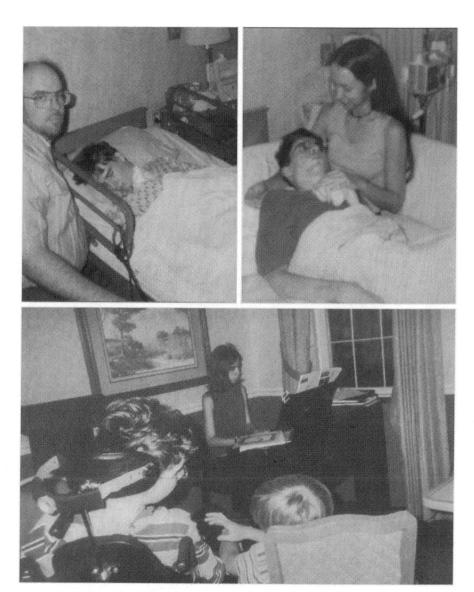

Top right: Melissa Brubaker visiting Jon in the nursing home. Bottom: Jon and Peter listening to Lauren play in the Common Room.

PART III

Coming Home

* * *

Comfort has its season but it's not in my air today.

No, today's the day for struggling and for reaching deep, they say.

It's the season of discomfort and for seeing the miles through.

Yes, the day will be filled with struggle; who I am is what I do,

In the long run.

– "THE LONG RUN" WORDS BY MARK KUNKEL

CHAPTER 18

October 17; Sunday
Dear Boys With Tools and Know-How and Generous Hearts:+

Mom told Jeff and me of your generous offer tonight of coming and helping to redo the bathroom. As we think of all the sacrifice that would involve, our hearts are full of love for you and your willing hearts and hands. We also realized that one of our "jobs" is to direct you as well as others around us that want to serve but just not sure how....

+[*Also known as my dad in Utah, brother Todd in Colorado, and brother-in-law Mark in Georgia.*]

October 24; Sunday
Dear Friends & Family:

...Looking ahead, Dr. Polin (Jonathan's rehab doctor that has been with him from the very beginning) wants the baclofen pump trial scheduled ASAP. The highest dose of baclofen still isn't giving us the desired results. If all goes well, Jonathan should have the pump by the time he comes home. I continue to prepare for that time by meeting with contractors and plumbers for bids, therapists for teaching and advice, a case manager for coordinating it all, and on Wednesday Jeff and I will meet with the United Cerebral Palsy (UCP) agent.+ Fortunately in the past few years, UCP has expanded to include brain injuries, so it looks like they will be a great resource as they handle any government money we get in the form of a waiver. This can then be used for remodeling our bathroom and getting aides to assist us with Jon's care. We have been very blessed to not have to pay for anything yet as far as his care goes. That will change somewhat when he comes home, but it certainly could be worse.

+[*A few years later UCP will change its name to United Disabilities Services (UDS), a nonprofit organization that, eight years later, will play an even bigger role in our lives.*]

October 28; Thursday (Note from my husband)
Hi Nettie!

I wanted to drop you a quick note and let you know that I hope you're doing okay with your mom being gone now. That we have such strong emotions about saying goodbye is a wonderful sign that the family ties and bonds are strong, and that our lives have been lived in a way that deep joy and wonderful relationships are possible.... The same depth of love that causes us so much worry for Jonathan has also strengthened us as we have found comfort in the arms of others....

Jeff

November 7; Sunday

Dear Friends & Family:

I'm going to ignore the fact that it is now midnight, for I don't want another day to go by without letting you in on what's been going on here. Jonathan spent Tuesday through Friday of this past week here at Lancaster General Hospital getting the trial for the baclofen pump. The neurosurgeon approved the surgery for the pump and scheduled it for November 19. This will involve implanting a catheter and pump (the size of a hockey puck) into Jon's abdomen. The pump stores a 3-month supply of baclofen that will get refilled as long as he needs it. When he no longer needs it, then they can go in and remove it. We're hoping that this will loosen Jonathan's legs and arms up so that he's more comfortable and will have an easier time regaining the use of his extremities.

This is all quite amazing considering it's a fairly new procedure for coma patients. If Jonathan had to go into a coma, I'm glad it was now and not 10 years ago. Despite doctors' understanding of TBI's being in infancy stage, they've still come a long way in these past 10 years.

So when should we bring Jonathan home? When do we have to? Or will he be ready for the TBI rehab? These are all questions that we fasted and prayed about today. We were reassured that as his progress unfolds, we will once again know what to do. The nursing home staff would like to keep an eye on him for that week after the pump, so the soonest we would bring him home now will be November 29. There is a possibility, however, that we could bring him home for a day pass on Thanksgiving Day.

Despite what it sounds like so far, life with Jonathan is not all decisions and technical stuff! We have been lifted up throughout these past five months with some very wonderful and powerful spiritual experiences and help from what we call our "earthly angels." But these past few weeks, we have been getting glimpses of the spiritual experience this has also been for Jonathan. His responses to questions and things we say have become easier to read and more frequent. Through a series of questions and answers, we are pleasantly surprised at: 1) his intellect being intact, 2) the help and comfort he has received from his own "heavenly angels," and 3) his increased testimony of Jesus Christ and His sacrifice for not only our sins but our infirmities as well. At first, this was quite amazing to me, but then I reminded myself that we have a perfectly loving Father in Heaven whose work and whose glory it is to bring us back to Him. So why deny Jonathan of the same comfort and guidance we're receiving just because he's in a coma? Certainly he's in a better position to receive it than me! Oh, the lessons we are learning from all of this.

November 9; Tuesday

Dear Annette:

I'm sorry that I wasn't able to give you a blessing last night. I had wanted to, but by the time we got everything wrapped up, it was late and I had gone into my wind down mode for the night. I would, however, like to do it tonight.

I am thankful that the Lord continually compensates for the down times in our lives. This situation with UCP has been somewhat of a roller coaster, with things going well, then things going not so well, then things going well again. Let's exercise our faith that the Lord is in control, and that He will direct things for our good and to His glory. I believe that there are things going on that we are unaware of at this time. Lives are being touched and the Lord's purposes are being fulfilled.

I had no idea what to expect when I went and visited Jon last night. Perhaps deep down inside, I was also somewhat skeptical that he would respond. It was a wonderful lift to have him respond so readily to me there in the lounge. It is difficult for me to express the feelings I had when he looked up at me after the blessing I gave him, a blessing of promised recovery and continued progress. I felt his love for me and expressed my deep love to him. I felt his deep yearning desire to express his feelings to me, and his concern and sadness at being unable to do so. He is a precious son of God that we are responsible for at this time. I have become closer to Jon and Jon to me. The walls of his privateness are being broken down as they could not have been done before. As I express my love to him, he doesn't shut off, but looks at me with all the effort he can, and I sense that he wants me to know that he is ready to accept us into his life.

The Lord touched me again this morning on my way to work with a deep sense of peace and a feeling that all will be all right. He is in control. I wept again this morning on the way to work, in gratitude for all that He has done for us, and that He has been very, very mindful of us in this situation.

I look forward to seeing you again tonight.

Love, Jeff

* * *

I am a child of God, and He has sent me here,
Has given me an earthly home with parents kind
and dear.
Lead me, guide me, walk beside me, help me find
the way.
Teach me all that I must do to live with Him
someday.

–"I AM A CHILD OF GOD" HYMN #301;
WORDS BY NAOMI WARD RANDALL

November 19; Friday afternoon. *Jonathan has made incredible progress this past week. It all started last Saturday, November 13, exactly five months since the accident. Jeff, Lauren, Peter, and I stopped in before heading over to the state band competition. Out of the blue, Jon smiled for his dad. It was a closed-mouth lopsided grin, but it was a smile! He did it for the rest of us, and you could tell he was quite proud of himself.*

Then on Sunday he was making noise for Grandma and Grandpa W. when they asked him to say words. On Monday I noticed that he was mouthing the words along as I sang "I Am a Child of God" to him. Wednesday was the big breakthrough. That morning while he was working with Patty, the occupational therapist, she could tell he was wanting to say something. Finally she said in frustration, "Jonathan, are you trying to tell me something?" and he said "Yes!" It not only surprised Patty, but Jon as well! Then throughout the morning's therapy, they were able to get him to repeat "yes" as well as one "no" and even a more muffled "Hi Beth." But by the time I got there that afternoon, he was too pooped to say anything for me. However, the next day – after giving him a day off of therapy because he told them to "go away" – he was pretty alert for me. I got him to repeat back whatever I asked of him with some words more intelligible than others. As I got ready to go, I tried to get him to say "bye Mom" but nothing. So I said, "Oh, never mind. Goodbye my dear." And then he said in that raspy voice that hasn't been used for five months, "Bye Mom." I guess he didn't want me to leave.

Today was the best, however. As I was trying to get him to talk for Marie the CNA, I had him repeat each word after me of "I love you Mom" which he did. Then Marie and I began talking until we heard him speaking. On his own he said, "I love you Mom." Wow! You can imagine how that made me feel! Not only did he get four words out on his own, but he wanted to tell me that. It not only touched me, but the news quickly spread to the staff who were also touched.

Something else he did today was cry. It was more of a vocal cry as opposed to a teary one. When he did it this morning, he indicated that his chest hurt. When he cried for me this afternoon, he said it was his head. Jeff and I suspect that as he becomes more aware of his situation, he's a bit scared by it all.

The other bit of news is that he did not get the baclofen pump surgery today. We found out only last night that the neurosurgeon's office canceled it last week when they got the word that it had been denied by our insurance for being "out-of-network." What this all means is that we'll probably have it done in York with an in-network neurosurgeon, but probably not until mid-December. This further complicates our decision on when to move Jonathan to the Mechanicsburg acute-level rehab. After all that we did to make this surgery happen, I'm beginning to wonder if it simply was not in the plan to have it done this week by Dr. Kuhlangel. Was it divine intervention or human error? Regardless, I have a feeling it will all turn out in the end.

As I see this miracle unfolding, I can't help but recall the words of Dr. Good, the neurologist who took care of him that first week. I remember our first family meeting and hearing him say, "The prognosis isn't good. There is definitely damage to the brain. He could get some back. He could be a vegetable the rest of his life. We just don't know." We got the distinct impression that he envisioned Jonathan wasting *away in a nursing home the rest of his life. Yet after five months and still progressing, he can speak! He can think. He can feel. And he can love. Dare I imagine what is next?*

November 23; Tuesday (Letter to Jon's former art professor at Southern Virginia College)

Dear Mrs. Crawford:

... Oh, how far he has come! Somehow I knew from the very beginning that my challenge in all this would not be the despair or the grief, but rather the patience needed for this very long road. Some days I find it difficult to leave my home and family to visit Jonathan. But just as difficult <u>is</u> to leave Jonathan for my home and family. It's a struggle to maintain both of my "homes," but the strain is made tolerable as I am so often surrounded by caring, upbeat, and loving people. It also helps tremendously to take time for myself – usually in the form of a good book or singing at the piano. But probably the greatest factor in keeping me going is the overwhelming trust I have in my Father in Heaven's wisdom and love. One of our beautiful hymns comes to mind:

I will not doubt, I will not fear; God's love and strength are always near.

His promised gift helps me to find an inner strength and peace of mind.

I give the Father willingly my trust, my prayers, humility.
His spirit guides; his love assures that fear departs when faith endures.

-"When Faith Endures" Hymn #128; text by Naomi W. Randall

CHAPTER 19

November 25; Thanksgiving Day

Dear Friends & Family:

Is it possible that I can top last week's news? How about this one – Jonathan can read! To think that we've gone from simply being able to do a thumbs up to reading and saying words. Definitely a miracle in the making. Here's how we found out....

Jonathan was having terrible abdominal spasms yesterday, so he was taken to York Hospital's ER for further tests. The two of us were there for about five hours, mostly waiting for results. Fortunately in between the spasms he was pretty alert and cooperative, so we practiced with his speech. When we weren't doing that, I would sing to him or read the *Reader's Digest* I happened to take along. As I was going through my bag to see what else we could do, I noticed that Jeff had written on the note pad "Raise your eyebrows." We've tried previously to see if Jonathan could read without success. Being somewhat bored, I thought it worth a shot again. This time he raised his eyebrows when I showed the paper to him! So I tried another one that read, "Wink." He then raised his eyebrows again. Rats. I wasn't ready to give up, though. I then wrote, "Hi Mom" knowing that he could say those words clearly. This time I asked him to tell me what it said and he said it back! Word after word he repeated back to me, graduating to "Hi, how are you?" I could tell he was as pleased with himself as I was!

We finally did find out that he has a bad urinary tract infection. The good news was that he could still come home today for Thanksgiving, but it will take a few days for the spasms to subside. So today didn't turn out quite as happy for him as we hoped, but in a way that might have been a blessing for him. With the spasms and not being quite as responsive today, he didn't seem to mind going back to the nursing home as much as if he had been more aware of the situation. We did find out that we can take care of him at home, but we will be glad that we'll get plenty of hours of help from attendants through UCP. He did manage to eat a few bites of cranberry sauce and mashed potatoes before the pain was too much and we had to lie him down again (on an air mattress in the living room). He did manage a "hi" and "bye" to his Aunt Trisha and friend Darren who called and talked to him via phone. All in all, I'd say it will be one of our most memorable and unique Thanksgiving days.

Okay. It's time I finally answered the Big Question, "So, is Jonathan still in a coma?" This has perplexed me as much as anyone, for no one has ever said, "He's out of the coma!" Back in October, I remember asking the question to the therapists and getting the reply, "Not until he's fully responsive." But then a few weeks ago, I asked the nursing home doctor and he said, "Why sure! When he opened his eyes he got out of the coma." Huh? I decided to watch the coma special that was on the Discovery channel again and their definition was like the doctor's – when eyes are open and he's responsive to his surroundings. The therapists weren't totally wrong, however. When using the Rancho scale of 1-8, the agitated level 4 is usually thought of as "breaking through the coma." With all this in mind, I asked Jon's speech therapist this week where he was on that scale. "Oh, he's still at a level 3." Huh? How can that be? Here are my unscientific yet up-close-and-personal conclusions:

Jonathan did come out of his coma when he opened his eyes and started responding to simple commands. His condition now can be termed "recovering from TBI (traumatic brain injury). The Rancho scale is useless in cases like Jonathan's where the progress is so slow. When Jeff and I reread over the descriptions of each level, Jon fluctuates between levels 2-5.

So when do we send him to the TBI rehab in in Mechanicsburg? After asking this to his physiatrist, Dr. Polin, he said any time after the baclofen pump is put in. And when will that be? We'll know that after his December 3 consultation with a new neurosurgeon, Dr. Winer.

The other question some of you have asked is, "How are his siblings handling all of this?" It's so easy to take for granted just how well they are dealing with nursing homes, wheelchairs, a handicapped brother, and an uncertain future. But sometimes I step back and am amazed. I look and see Andrew popping wheelies in Jon's wheelchair in the family room today. I see his willingness, even desire, to go and help maneuver him in and out of the van as well. I see Peter wanting to go to the nursing home any chance he can get. I also see him lying next to him or reading scriptures to him or just giving him one of his pep talks. I see Lauren (who is afraid of so many things in life) *not* afraid to be in the nursing home with its sometimes strange smells, strange people, and strange situations. I see her playing the piano freely at the nursing home. Because of this unexpected situation and their positive approach, our children have increased in tolerance, selflessness, and compassion. It's wonderful!

On this day of thanks, I truly am thankful that I don't have to look back on this year and see the passing of a child. Rather, there is such hope for the future and a past full of small but oh so significant miracles. Isn't life great!

With my love and gratitude for each of you,
Annette

December 2; Thursday night. *Yesterday was a bit gut wrenching for me. Once again I heard Jonathan say, "Mom. Home." And once again I explained why he couldn't go home just yet. And then later as I got ready to leave it was, "Mom. Stay here." Oh, and such pleading in his voice! I tried to explain that I needed to leave so I could sing in my Grandview Singers concert, but somehow that responsibility didn't seem so important anymore. But still, I tried to leave. As I did, I heard him yelling, "Mom, Mom!" I came back and reassured him that he would be okay. As I walked down the hallway, however, I heard him again yelling, pleading my name. Once again, a few tears were spilled on the way home.*

December 9; Thursday

Dear Friends & Family:

What a week! It began last Friday with the long awaited consultation with the new neurosurgeon, Dr. Winer, regarding Jon's baclofen pump surgery. As soon as I met him and shook his hand, I began to think that maybe *this* was the way it was supposed to happen after all. As we had a non-rushed visit, I not only was impressed with his bedside manner, but also his expertise. Apparently, he was one of the doctors that helped with pump research prior to FDA approval in 1981. When I told him about how the other doctor mistakenly canceled the surgery, as well as our desire to have it done as soon as possible, he said he'd see what he could do. Then I overheard him say to one of his staff, "Call the hospital and see if tomorrow morning is possible." Whoa! Wow! He just happened to be on call at the hospital that weekend and he just happened to have another patient cancel, so by 4:50 pm the surgery was all arranged. We just didn't know where Jon was going from there. Earlier in the week, someone from Healthsouth Rehab in Mechanicsburg had evaluated him, approved him, but said they needed to wait for a bed to open up.

Another real blessing that weekend was Megan's timely visit. She's a dear friend of Jonathan's from

Southern Virginia College who came to visit one more time before moving back to Utah. What a help she was to stay with Jonathan and calm all of his fears while I would be answering a zillion questions at the doctor's office and at the hospital. Jonathan is now quite aware of his surroundings, but with very little short-term memory, he can't figure out why he is strapped to the skinny ambulance bed, or why he can't go home, or why he can't get up and walk....

The surgery went very well. The pump was inserted under his skin above his waist line in the right abdomen. Eighty-seven micrograms of baclofen are now continually flowing and telling his muscles to release and relax. That amount will be adjusted over the next 4-5 weeks up to 2000 mg until they figure out the right dosage for him. All this is done via a computer chip in the pump. Cool, huh? What's not so cool is that he'll more than likely need this the rest of his life unless they invent something even better. Already, though, we've noticed less tension, particularly in his legs.

Jonathan continued to stay in York Hospital until Tuesday morning when he was cleared to go to Healthsouth. At last! The long anticipated acute rehab! The average stay is 30 days, but because Jonathan has healed at a slower rate, they're figuring 45-60 days. And *then* he can come home! The rehab is about two minutes from Jeff's work and about 50-60 minutes from home.

What is Jonathan like these days? In some ways, he's like a child. He can understand quite clearly, but accepts all with childlike faith and innocence. He's quite gentle and loving. He can also be a cry baby! For example, when Jeff went in two nights ago, he was crying that his legs hurt while taking a shower. It appeared they had gone to sleep, but he didn't understand that. Then his nose got stuffed up while in the shower, and he was yelling, "I can't breathe! Help!" Fortunately for me, the next night when I came in I got the sweet gentle side. Yes, he shows his negative emotions, but he also shows the positive ones. His face so easily lights up with brightness in his eyes and that crooked smile of his. He will spontaneously tell Jeff or me "I love you," and there is such sincerity when he does so. My favorite part of last night's visit, though, was our "show and tell" time. What a delight to share with him the CD his Uncle Mark just made for him with songs that Jonathan has created and sung over the past few years, then see his reaction when I tell him, "That's you singing, Jonathan!" Or sharing the CD of Zach Bailey's "Brown Derby Junction" and say, "Your friend wrote this song." Or just before hanging his Christmas stocking, telling him that his Grandma W. made it for him. His reaction is always one of surprise, awe, and an audible, "Ohhhhh....!" And the "wonderful" thing about having a messed up short term memory is that we can do this all over again today and he won't remember! His long term is a bit better, but it's as if someone took an egg beater and scrambled up all that memory pack of his. But it is improving with time. We've been asking him certain questions each day to see what he can remember from day to day. His answers seem to be getting more accurate. For example, when asked how much he weighs, he's gone from "320 lbs." to more recently "140 lbs." (He started out at 127 lbs. and left Manor Care at 103 lbs. Not too good for someone almost 6 feet tall.)

I love sharing this unfolding miracle with all of you, our dear friends and family. I simply hope and pray that someday this might help you with whatever trials you may face. I recall a talk given in church a while ago entitled, "Into the Woods and Out Again." As the speaker cited accounts of people in fairy tales and in scriptures being taught, refined, and purified while wandering in their wilderness, I saw clearly how I would someday face my own wilderness experience. I just had no idea it would involve my son being in a coma. And who knows how many more woods I'll have to face until my earthly journey is over? This I do know. I can do it!

Not alone, but with family, friends, and a loving – oh so loving – Father in Heaven.

CHAPTER 20

December 9; Thursday night at Healthsouth Rehab. Jonathan and I have thoroughly enjoyed each other's company tonight. He is so expressive, through his words and smiles, of his love for me. When I asked him what I could do for him, he replied, "Sing for me." That's easy! I loved lying next to him singing "Angel" and "How Firm a Foundation." Do you see why I'm enjoying this bond that we now have? He has the innocence of a child yet the understanding of an adult. He has a simplicity now without the baggage.

It didn't take long to trust the staff and this place. They are well staffed and caring. I will miss our "family" at Manor Care, but not the smells, the soaked-through diapers, or the alarms on the doors. The big question is, what will he be like? One step at a time, Annette. One day at a time.

December 10; Friday evening . *I got to the rehab today just as the occupational therapist was giving Jonathan an eye test... and they didn't even know he wore glasses! Needless to say, he did better with the glasses on. It was good to finally meet the therapists and share a bit about Jonathan. Unlike the other places he's been, Healthsouth is not as dependent upon the family for his care and therapy. And they're more concerned about maintaining a quiet, distraction free environment. I still feel visits are important, but I also want Jon to develop trusting relationships with the staff. It's okay, though; I <u>really</u> need more time at home.*

December 13; Monday afternoon. *Today is the 6-month anniversary since the accident. I'm not sure if it's the rainy weather, the anniversary, or just time for my weekly cry, but it's really gotten to me today. Here's what my head and heart are saying:*

Why am I crying? Well, for starters I had a son almost die six months ago. Yeah, but look how it's turned out. This has been a six-month spiritual journey that I will always cherish. Besides, what was Jonathan's future before the accident? Yes, he was preparing for a church mission, but could he have made it the whole two years without a mental breakdown or his mental illness getting in the way? Then beyond his mission, would he have been one of those "starving artists" dependent upon his parents to bail him out between sales?

Would he have found the right one to marry that could keep his life and finances on track?

Jon's future has completely changed, and so have the questions. Will he be able to provide for himself and a family? Find someone who will look beyond whatever disabilities remain? Considering that our earth life is but a dot on the eternal lifeline, I am more than happy to have these new concerns, for I now know that the Lord has a keen interest in seeing that Jonathan fulfills his other mission here on earth... whatever that may be.

December 18; Saturday

Dear Friends & Family:

Jonathan's greatest achievement this week has been going from eating pureed food to just about anything! Not bad for a kid that was getting fed through a stomach tube just two weeks ago. Apparently, he's forgotten what he didn't like to eat, and eats everything they put in front of him and still wants more! He's also able to feed himself with just a bit of help. He only has the use of his right pointer and thumb, but it's amazing what he can do with just those two fingers.

His other big accomplishment is learning to steer for himself in a powered wheelchair. I had to ask his physical therapist, "So Melanie, I know he's not going to leave here walking, but will he ever be able to?" Our discussion led to the conclusion that it would be difficult because of all his physical impairments, but don't discount it. The way I see it, we'll plan as if he'll never walk again while being absolutely thrilled if he does!

Other impairments we're just finding out from tests being done: Jonathan has severe damage to his hearing in the left ear. He also has some damage to his left eye while being difficult to focus on one particular object in his right eye. His long-term memory is fairly good, but he usually doesn't remember anything from day to day, even hour to hour. I'm not sure why, but finding all this out didn't seem too terribly distressing. Maybe it's because he still <u>can</u> hear, and see, and remember at least his first 18 years of life.

Jonathan continues to endear himself to the staff and his visitors with his gentleness, politeness, and intelligence. My favorite "Jonathan Saying of the Week": Just out of the blue he said, "Mom, is there anything I can do for you?" He continues to plead "Take me home...NOW!" and finding all kinds of creative ways to ask. The other day he asked the nurse if she had a car. When she replied yes, he then said, "Then take me home!" Apparently, this fixation on going home is normal for TBI rehabs. It's all part of the confusion and certainly not a reflection of the wonderful care he gets there.

I've had many ask me if I've been able to do any Christmas this year. As I thought about this, I have to answer that the shopping, giving, concerts, and parties have all been kept to a minimum, but my appreciation, understanding, and love for the Savior – who is the reason for Christmas – has grown tremendously. The one thing I get plenty of time for is pondering as I drive back and forth, and I've done plenty of pondering about the role of Jesus Christ in all of this and His incredible love for us. So, yes, I guess I have had time to "do" Christmas this year! May this find all of you pondering, worshiping, and loving our Savior and Redeemer.

With love and good wishes for this Christmas season.

December 19; Sunday night. *Went and saw Jonathan tonight with Peter and Jeff. We first caught a glimpse of him in the activity room eating his supper. He had food all over his bib and food on his mouth. I suppose that to anyone else, the scene would have been embarrassing or even pathetic. But I found it endearing. The thought of Jonathan being handicapped – physically and/or mentally – for the rest of his life doesn't scare me like I thought it would. I guess I've seen this too much as a spiritual journey to feel otherwise.*

Here's a summary of tonight's conversations with Jonathan....

The nurse mentioned that Santa came in to see all the patients. Jonathan asked Santa, "Where's my present?" Santa: "Well now, it's not December 25th yet." Jon: "Then take me home." He's even hitting on Santa for that one!

Jon to his dad while lying in bed: "Dad, tell me a story." Dad: "Once upon a time there was a little boy who was dearly loved...." And from there he proceeded to give a very brief summary of Jon's life up to and including the car accident.... "And that boy who was loved so much is you, Jonathan." Jon: "Really? Wow...."

For the umpteenth zillionth time, Jon: "Dad, take me home." Dad: "No Jonathan, you need to get better." But this time, Jon said: "How?" Dad: "Well, for one thing you need to learn how to walk." Jon: "Oh, I can already do that." Dad: "Then show me." Jonathan then proceeded to try and get out of his wheelchair, but to no avail. But instead of getting frustrated, he simply said, "I'll show you tomorrow."

Yesterday Jonathan laughed a real laugh for the first time since the accident when Jeff had him repeat the phrase, "Peter is stinky." He thought that was so funny! He also sang tonight right along with Jeff, "I Am a Child of God." This time, he was able to get most of the words out. I thought back on the time that Jeff and I sang that song to him in the trauma unit. And now to hear him sing that fervent plea, "Lead me, guide me, walk beside me; help me find the way...." It really touched my heart, as I'm sure it did his Father in Heaven's.

December 20; Monday night

More Ways to Say, "Take Me Home" by Jonathan Whitlock

- _Take Andrew and me home._
- _Let's go to Pizza Hut for dinner._
- _Please... (and a big smile)_
- _I'm cold. As Jeff gets a blanket, "No, I want my jacket."_
- _Take me to my dorm room._
- _To the nurse, "How are you doing today?" "Fine, Jonathan." "Then take me home."_
- _I am not fixated on going home. I swear I am not fixated. Now take me home!_

January 2, 2000; Sunday

Dear Friends & Family:

Will life get "back to normal" now that Christmas is past and the new year is here? After doing the "Jonathan thing" for half of 1999, I wonder just what _is_ normal? It's funny, but as much as I enjoyed my life before the accident I don't yearn for those days as much as I look forward to the days of progress and change that lie ahead of us. This literally has been a life changing experience for all of us... and I say that in a positive way!

As visible progress has slowed, however, there are those days that I begin to lose a bit of my trust to doubts with Jon's progress. What if he can't ever remember from day to day? What if his hand coordination never comes back? Will he always be totally dependent on others?

How do I fight these worrisome thoughts? Two things. First, by recalling all the reassurances of the Spirit that there *is* a loving Father in Heaven's plan being implemented with His perfect timing. And second, by visiting with Jonathan. His conversations are full of love and gratitude for us as well as the little things life is offering him. Yes, he has a few questions repeated over and over, but he also has a sense of humor and an unusual insight and perspective. In other words, he's really quite pleasant to be around. My brother Todd and his family from Georgia noticed this during their visit this past week. As Todd said, "There's a good feeling in that room." And besides all this, I don't have to worry about Jonathan's driving anymore nor his late night hours! But for the most part, I continue to be full of faith and hope and gratitude for this opportunity to learn some very important lessons from life.

Our Christmas was... well, a bit unusual. After a traditional morning of opening presents, we packed up the kids and the gifts that we gave Jonathan and he gave us (thanks to Mom and Dad doing his shopping), and made the one-hour trip to the rehab. What fun to see Jonathan absolutely amazed at receiving his few gifts and hearing his sincere appreciation! He did a pretty good job guessing just by the wrapped shape what he was giving to each of us. We camped out in his room for the whole afternoon before heading home for our very nontraditional dinner – leftover enchiladas. (Oh well!) Sadly Jonathan couldn't remember any of this the following day.

Another way Jonathan's thinking process is messed up is his fear that this is all a dream. Along with the ever present questions of, "When can I go home?" is "If I fall asleep, will you wake me up?" Wouldn't you think that he *would* want this to be a dream that he could wake up from? I'm glad that he doesn't think that way, for we can honestly assure him that yes, this is reality. "But Mom, what can I do to prove to myself that this is reality?" Bittersweet, isn't it?

January 4; Tuesday

Annette:

I've been putting together a list of logistical items for us to prepare for Jon coming home. The following is that list. Could you please let me know if you have any things to add to it?

- Locate source of Texas catheters including tubes, bags, skin prep, leg straps.
- Buy disposable briefs (small Depends work okay).
- Medications–need to get list and get prescriptions. Need training on how to administer them. Need to review with doctor and determine if we can delete any.
- Feeding – Need to make sure we have guidelines on feeding Jon and how to record calories. Do we need any kitchen equipment to chop or puree food? Need to understand what kind of meals we need to prepare for "Jon the Bottomless Pit."
- Fluids – Need guidelines on making sure Jon gets proper fluids and how to record them.
- Need to get durable equipment rented and delivered – bed, wheelchair, bed transfer lift.
- Need syringes and any other items for peg tube feeding; training and guidelines on how to use.
- Get ramps.

Buy:
  - bed sheets for hospital bed
  - several pillows; washable?
  - washable and disposable bed pads
  - suppositories; need training for bowel program

- ○ wash basin and tearless shampoo for bed baths
- ○ disposable bibs for feeding
- ○ something to cover the floor in the living room in case of throwing up

The list above is a long list of things that need to be done. I want you to know that you will not be doing this alone. I can take time off to help us transition, and I think that there will be other help that will come as needed. I want the kids to also assist in Jon's care as they are able. This really needs to have the involvement of the whole family.

Looking forward to seeing you at 2:00 today –
Jeff

January 18; Tuesday

Dear Friends & Family:

Another two weeks has gone by and our spirits continue to stay upbeat. It's hard not to be when it's just plain fun to visit Jonathan every day! (I must admit books on tape have helped me with even enjoying the two-hour round trip.)

We have a definite date when Jonathan will be home – Thursday, February 3rd. Two weeks from Thursday! It's quite a relief to finally be given a concrete date. It makes it much easier to *not* procrastinate getting the pillows, sheets, bed pads, etc. Also, much of Jeff's and my time these next two weeks will be devoted to learning how to take care of him at home. This all seems a little deja vu, perhaps because it reminds me of preparing to bring home our first newborn – Jonathan. Just as I was anxious to have the pregnancy behind me at 8 ½ months, that's kind of how I feel again. Hey, instead of a 9-month ordeal, however, it will only have been 8 months!

News flash: Jon's stomach peg tube is gone! He's not throwing up so much, but it's still an occasional problem. He can now eat regular food! Getting the food into his mouth is still awkward with only the use of his right thumb and index finger, but he still loves to pack it in. And finally, there are flashes of retaining short term memory. For instance, the dog he wants us to get to eat the scraps that fall to the floor during his messy meal times is a "wiener dog." To remember this latter bit of info, Jeff had him repeat, "I want a wiener dog" five times in a row. Jonathan thought this was pretty dumb, and sure enough, by the fifth time he said instead, "I want a palm tree (snicker, snicker)." But it worked; he's remembered it thus far! Today, as I was showing him the pictures from the photo album we've kept of his ordeal he exclaimed, "Oh, I thought this was all a bad dream." I asked him if he remembered being at the hospital and nursing home and he said, "Barely. It's way deep in the back of my mind." Interesting....

To help Jonathan remember and perhaps not ask so many repetitive questions, Jeff typed up a paper that we'll be posting in his rehab room. It includes his daily schedule, where he is, when he'll be going home, and when he gets to see his family. It must be hard to wake up *every* morning and have so little clue as to where you are or why you're here. As you can tell, his family is so very important to him right now. It's quite fun to see his face light up when we walk in that door!

One story I want to share with you. Way back in the beginning of all of this, nine-year-old Peter got the idea that it would be nice for Jonathan to have a pet bird to keep him company when he would get home. (Jonathan's cockatiel, VJ, had passed away shortly after he went off to college.) So Peter determined to save up his allowance and buy a parakeet for him. (At $70, cockatiels were out of his price range.) I had called the shop owner where we had gotten VJ to see if she had any hand-fed parakeets since we needed a very tame one. She remembered Jonathan and promised to keep the best of the litter for him that was due around Christmas. Well, I kept procrastinating calling her until last week. She said they were still there, but to come in soon. When we came in two days later, she asked Peter if he wouldn't mind having a cockatiel instead of a parakeet. I explained that he only had $34. "No," she said, "This bird is free... to a good home." Apparently, shortly after I called her, the owner of this particular cockatiel called her and asked if she could find a good home for her very tame gray male named Marcel since she was moving and couldn't take him with her. The shop owner immediately thought of Jonathan. What a perfect match for Jon's needs! Jonathan will be able to hold Marcel on his left hand and stroke him with the two good fingers on his right hand. What is the likelihood of getting a free cockatiel already tamed?! By the way, Peter ended up spending his money on a cage there at the shop. Do you suppose there was a bit of divine intervention on behalf of a selfless and loving brother's intentions?

To close, I just want to say thanks to all of you who are writing Jonathan. If possible, could you include a picture of yourself? He remembers faces right now better than names.

Despite becoming more aware of his circumstances (showers are now "embarrassing"), he continues to bear all things with patience and a sense of humor. We feel so very blessed that he's made it this far and look forward to witnessing what time will heal... and a little hard work on his part!

CHAPTER 21

January 30; Sunday

Dear Friends & Family:

FOUR more days until our Jonathan is home!! Sometimes that still seems like an eternity to Jon ("Can I go home *now*?"), and other times we get the "Oh, WOW!" Our free time is now focused on preparing for the Big Day. Jeff thinks of all the little details and, for the most part, I do the shopping, phone calling, and talking. (I say "for the most part" since I can't forget our Friday night date at WalMart where he found a pack of 18 washcloths for 90 cents.)

Yes, there are many details, but we're getting a lot of help and ideas. There's the nursing staff who patiently answers all of our questions. How often do we turn Jon at night? How is the bowel program working? What should we expect of the home health workers? Then there's Becca, our case manager/social worker who is taking care of setting up the therapists, getting the equipment approved and delivered, helping us fill out forms for a handicapped parking sticker, approval for bus transportation, etc. Then there's the therapists at Healthsouth who are teaching us how to transfer from bed to wheelchair or from wheelchair to car, and who help us figure out just the right shower chair. Then there's Tracey at church who volunteered to help line up the volunteers for that pre-attendant care time and who is watching out for my mental health. ("By the way, Annette, don't forget about you and Jeff needing some time alone.") Then there's the Lord who brings a sweet peace and calm over all of this and reminds us that He will not give us more than we can handle. ("Don't forget that Jonathan is my son and I love him, too.")

And then there's *you* with your encouraging notes, your letters to Jonathan, your advice, and your prayers. I would like to share with you one such example from Jonathan's Uncle Mark. A few years ago he wrote a poem he entitled, "The Long Run." He included it in a recent CD that he made of his original songs and introduced it with these words: "I wrote this as a poem following a 40th birthday 50-mile run in April of 1997, and later on my nephew Jon Whitlock wrote music for it and made this tape for me. Given his season of plodding and discomfort these days due to a serious head injury six months ago, I can hardly listen to him sing it... but need to. Here's to seasons of small victories, friend and brother Jonathan." I wish I could send you the music along with the words; he did such a nice job with it. Little did any of us dream that years later the message would take on a new dimension. Bittersweet and truly a treasure. [*Note: During his first year at home, we gathered all of Jonathan's songs he wrote, played, and recorded on a four-track recorder Mark gave to him. We gave them to Zach Bailey, a good friend of Jonathan's who happens to have a sound studio. He cleaned up the background noises as much as possible and put them together as a CD. We made copies and have been giving them out to friends, family, and all the new acquaintances he has met on his journey. Truly a treasure since Jonathan never completely regained his pre-accident voice.*]

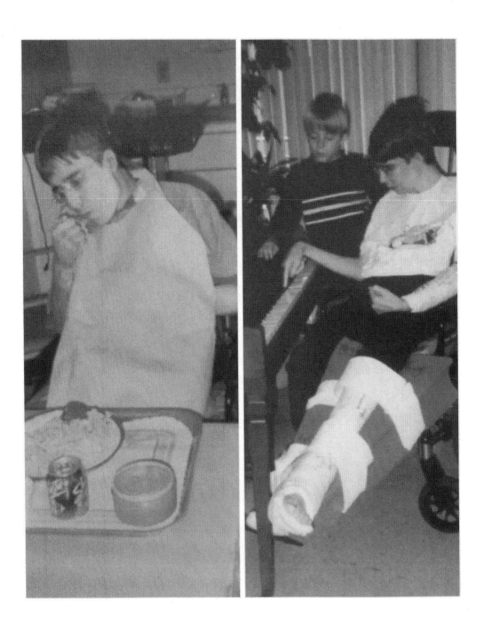

PART IV

Home & Beyond

* * *

Dreaming has its season and it's in my air today.
Yes, today's a day for going forth and
conquering, they say.
I'm heading towards my destiny and it's calling
out my name.
I don't know when I'll get there, but I'll get there
just the same,
In the long run.

– "THE LONG RUN" WORDS BY ZACH BAILEY

CHAPTER 22

March 8, 2000

Dear Friends & Family:

By now you are probably wondering if Jonathan's homecoming did us in. That's a good question. Some days I might answer, "Yep." Other days, "Almost, but not quite." And still others, "Hey, we're not doing too badly!"

Do you remember starting a new job and feeling a little overwhelmed by all the things you had to learn and all the things you didn't know? For the first few days, that's what it was like for Jeff and me. But soon we learned how best to dispense Jonathan's meds and get him in and out of bed; the best way to help him try and feed himself, shave, and brush his teeth; the shortcuts to bathing and dressing him; and how to answer his never-ending questions. What was – and still is – difficult to do is finding time for the other parts of our lives. We're still trying to figure out the best way to divide up "Jonathan tasks" among the family members. So far we have Lauren typing his journal as he dictates, Andrew turning him at 5:30 when he wakes up for Seminary*, and Peter helping him tape record. That only leaves me (and Jeff when he's home) with putting on and off the arm splints and leg brace; toilet training and bowel program; working with the therapists; doing his daily laundry, phone calls, transferring, feeding, bathing.... And for all of us, answering the never-ending questions.

Did I mention that Jonathan asks a lot of questions?! With little or no short-term memory, it can leave anyone a bit confused. At the rehab, it was always, "When will I see my family?" Now that he's at home, here are Jon's current "Top Ten Questions" asked over and over:
- What is wrong with me?
- Will I get better?
- When will I get all better?
- When will I see Melissa next?
- How old am I?
- Am I expected to go on a mission?
- Am I expected to be looking for a wife?
- Where are my friends?
- When will I get my memory back?
- When can I wear contact lenses again?

It didn't take long to come up with a question/answer sheet for him to refer to that helps somewhat.

One great blessing in all of this is that Jonathan's intellect, wit, and personality were left intact – not always the case in TBI's. To give you an example, let me share-with his permission and leaving out all the repetitions-excerpts from his February 11th journal entry:

Dear Jon –

Don't you remember any of this? What... you can't? I'll have to tell you what happened. You arrived home for the first time in a long time. You have ideas of what life is like. You love your family very much. You have a lot of ideas but no conclusions.... You're really scared about what will happen. But you love your home and your family. Jon, so get up and paint! You have a lot to do, and you don't know how you'll do it. You're really scared and you have to do everything for the first time. Of course, you forget a lot. In fact, you've forgotten what you're going to say!.... You can't see into the future, so I don't know how to react to this. Don't be so sad! Get up and get a glass of chocolate milk, and give each member of your family a big hug. You're so lucky to have them, and you can't wait for tomorrow. Since you're reading this, I wonder what the future is like.... SMILE! Now shut up and go to the living room and have some fun on the computer.... Anyway, okay, c-ya later!

-The past Jon

Life *is* tough for us right now. No doubt about it! Tougher than we've experienced thus far. We've had to make adjustments to our lives and sacrifice much. But there's a certain joy – even times of peace – that come with this special kind of service. We are learning and stretching and growing. But as difficult as it is to be the care *giver*, how difficult it must be to be the care *needer*. As tired and worn out as I get from working with Jonathan, I would never want to trade places with him. How confusing and scary and discouraging this must be for him. Hmm, in this way, his short-term memory is a blessing! All the past humiliation of dependence, all the physical pain, all the vomiting, all the fears are erased and each new day *is* a new start.

And for what it's worth, I'll close with just a few things I have learned to keep my sanity that I think could apply to any prolonged challenge we face in life:

1. Share responsibility as much as possible.
2. Don't gyp on sleep.
3. Take even just a half-hour a day for

yourself.

4. Fill your life with uplifting things.

5. Involve the Lord.

The last reminds me of a verse from the hymn, "Did You Think to Pray?" that has recently made an impression on Jeff and me:

When sore trials came upon you, did you think to pray?

When your soul was full of sorrow, balm of Gilead did you borrow at the gates of day?

Oh, how praying rests the weary!

Prayer will change the night to day.

So, when life gets dark and dreary, don't forget to pray.

("Did You Think to Pray?" Hymn #140; words by Mary A. Pepper Kidder)

CHAPTER 23

April 25, 2000

Dear Friends & Family:

Many changes since I last wrote, much in part to the terrific home therapy team:

Physical Therapy – Jon can now scoot up and down the stairs on his behind. This is a wonderful accomplishment since that means he can now get a real shower two times a week.

Occupational Therapy – Jonathan still has a lot of tone in his dominant left hand, so he's had to switch to doing everything with his right hand. Despite this, he manages to do a few oil paintings, feed himself rather nicely, and write using the computer.

Speech Therapy – I'm beginning to wonder if Jonathan will always have this soft, raspy voice. He still needs to be reminded to use his "strong voice" and to articulate. His mind and wit are so sharp, however. His memory is slowly improving. His favorite reading material is "Answers to Your Most Commonly Asked Questions," his journal, letters from friends, and "Calvin & Hobbes" books. He also enjoys looking through his old sketch books and photo albums.

Home Health Care – By April 9 Jonathan was toilet trained. Yay! By April 18 he was turning himself at night which meant that we no longer had to get up during the night. Yay again! And just this morning, the O.T. session involved him undressing, bed bathing, and dressing just about by himself. Of course it took over an hour, but what an accomplishment!

Our family continues to take this all in stride. One of the best strategies has been for the siblings to tease and joke and fool around with him. During these times, it's hard for Jon to get too down on himself. And if they get out of hand, it doesn't take Jon too long to get one of them in a head lock! His positive attitude and sense of humor are contagious. There are days, however, that the stress and/or reality of the situation sneaks up on us. For instance, one day last week Peter came up to me fighting back the tears and said, "Mom, sometimes it hurts inside to see Jonathan. I remember what he used to be like...." What ultimately gives us the comfort and hope to go forward is our faith. Faith in a Savior whose resurrection makes it possible for Jonathan to be resurrected with a perfect physical body. Faith in a

Father in Heaven who provides us the necessary trials and opportunity to return to Him again. Faith that there is a purpose to all of this.

CHAPTER 24

May 20, 2000

    Dear Friends & Family:

    Jonathan's financial waiver finally kicked in! UCP can now provide attendant care for 40 hours per week! This will lift a huge burden off of our shoulders. Still, though, it's a bit unnerving to invite just anyone into our home for that many hours. Fortunately, Jon's new attendant isn't just anyone. Her name is Heather Hite, a 19-year-old who we know from church and who also has been working for UCP since she moved here from Utah back in December.

    Another big change comes this Monday when Jonathan will begin outpatient therapy at a day rehab facility about 15 minutes from our house. Whenever Jonathan moves to a different facility and group of therapists, he always makes a leap forward. I'm sure it will be no different this time.

In the meantime, Jonathan continues to progress slowly. Thinking about what he does when he's not doing therapy, I just asked Jeff what Jon's favorite activity is, and he replied, "Asking questions." Okay, this calls for another Top Ten List....

"Top Ten Things Jon Likes to Do in His Spare Time"

- Ask questions.
- Visit with Melissa.
- Read.
- Wrestle with his siblings.
- Say something funny and then "lose it" uncontrollably – either from his own dumb jokes or listening to his dumb laugh!
- Write poetry on the computer.
- Listen to Ben Folds Five or the CD of his own original music.
- Eat snacks that don't require wearing the "Insulting Bib." (We prefer calling it by its PC name – Clothing Protector.)
- Read letters and emails.
- Paint or look at paintings.

There you have it folks. If you didn't look over this past year, you might think, "Hey, that's not such a bad life!" Perhaps I should also include the Top Ten Dislikes....

"Top Then Things Jon Dislikes Doing In His Spare Time"

1. Hand stretches.
2. Standing up. ("Mom, that wheelchair sure looks inviting....")
3. Not remembering what was just said.
4. Having Mom shave what he missed on his face.
5. Having no privacy. ("Mom, let me just say that I'm glad you're not a pervert.")
6. Wearing that Insulting Bib.
7. Getting around in a wheelchair.
8. Taking his anti-constipation medicine, lactulose, a.k.a. "nectar of the gods" according to his dad. Ha!
9. Not having his normal voice.
10. Not knowing the future. ("When will I be done with this insulting lifestyle?")

July 6, 2000

Dear Friends & Family:

At last! A quiet moment for me to attempt to consolidate the last two months. In some ways a lot has happened and in other ways very little. Heather has now been with us for six weeks. I hope the memory of getting up early each morning to help Jon bathe, dress, and eat will never fade. As long as that happens, I know

I will never take Heather for granted. Not only does she take care of his personal needs, but she often gets him to therapy, and spends up to three hours a day doing the arm and leg stretches that the therapists are requesting. Ah, and I can't forget all the times she transfers him in and out of his chair. There's still plenty for the family to do, but she has certainly been a great asset.

Probably the biggest disappointment we have recently faced is Jonathan's lack of progress physically. Going from a very forward thinking, risk taking, progressive and loving home therapy team to a standard out-patient physical rehab center was not the best thing for Jonathan, but unfortunately necessary because of insurance reasons. With that said, please don't think we're discouraged. Jeff and I had a good talk about it the other day. The reality of the situation is that, medically speaking, Jonathan will only go so far – be it home therapists or out-patient therapists. When all has then been done for him physically, he will still fall short in many areas. But it simply doesn't matter how far he goes with the therapists' help. God will be able to heal him no matter if he's all bent up with tight muscles or walking with a cane. What does matter is that all involved do their best with what skills and time they have available. Then, when the time is right – whether it be in a month, a year, ten years, the millennium*,

Jon's life time, or the resurrection – Jonathan will be healed 100%. What a beautiful blessing and gift from our Savior! Coming to this knowledge has made it so much easier for me to be patient.

Just took a break to say goodnight to Jon and heard this exchange between a teasing father and his son:

Jon: What's wrong with me?

Dad: Well, let me tell you....

Jon (snickering): Besides drooling and belching.

Dad: You tell me – what's wrong with you?

Jon (snickering again): My father!

Two significant dates have recently passed. Jonathan spent his 19th birthday last year in the trauma unit still pretty much in a coma but surrounded by his friends. His 20th birthday on July 2nd was a bit more normal. Where do you suppose he wanted to go to celebrate? The Taj Mahal Restaurant of course! No matter how many times we asked him what he wanted to do, the Taj was always it.

The other significant date was June 13th. The one-year anniversary passed without too much fanfare outwardly, but inside this ole' mom it was pretty tough. Somehow, without my knowing it, I had subconsciously set a one-year deadline in my mind for my "enduring to the end" to be over. It took a big cry to get over it, but I did get over it and, once again, learned much from the experience. While I was an emotional basket case, Jeff was just the opposite. He was able to look back and see just how blessed our family and those around us have been because of this trial.

It truly has been an incredible year – a year of miracles, of love, of service, of change. I think we've all been changed for the good because of this journey. That is probably the first of many miracles that Jonathan may have seen when he chose to finish his life's journey here. Thank you again for taking the road with us and for continuing to do so as we "wait upon the Lord."+

+ *From Isaiah 40:31, "But they that wait upon the Lord shall renew their strength; they shall mount up with wings as eagles; they shall run, and not be weary; and they shall walk, and not faint."*

September 3, 2000

Dear Friends & Family:

I don't know about you, but I need these "Jonathan Updates." To me, it's like taking a moment on a long journey to look back on the road just traveled. Have you ever done that? There's great satisfaction in seeing what has been accomplished. And there's a new perspective with just a touch of hindsight. In these past few months, the scenery hasn't changed as often, probably because Jon's progress has slowed down. But there is still forward motion. For that we are grateful. We were told recently that most progress for brain injuries is done within two years, but the brain can continue to heal for another seven or more years. In addition to that, we also know that "with God nothing shall be impossible." (Luke 1:37)

While there has not been much progress with PT, OT, and speech, his cognitive therapy is doing quite well. He really works well with Michelle, his cognitive therapist that comes to the home on Fridays for two hours. Michelle bought him a whole bunch of thinking/memory type games and activities that he just loves to do. Jon may not get too excited about active range-of-motion exercises, but he sure loves to play Scrabble.

So where do we go from here once he's discharged? What UCP and his physiatrist are recommending is a post-acute rehab. Unfortunately, Acadia, the one in Lancaster would be a lateral move, comparable to what he's doing now, and was not recommended. The only other ones "nearby" are all in the Philadelphia area. Jon would live there for about six months doing more therapy with the goal of learning to live as independently as possible. We're a bit leery of the whole idea since it would be taking away the things most precious to Jon right now – family and familiar surroundings. He does *not* like the idea of living with "people like me" and away from home. We will look into it, however, with the hope that if it is the right thing to do, the Spirit will let us know.

In the meantime, the bathroom is *finally* being built. In just a few more weeks, Jonathan will be able to actually brush his teeth and spit in a sink, sit on a toilet, and take real showers every day! How many of us take these routine things for granted? Once the bathroom is completed and the bills are paid, then we'll move on to the bedroom. At least that's the plan.

As Jon's pace of progress slows down and we settle into a comfortable routine, the challenge has been to not get too complacent in our faith and expectations. It's easier to say, "We can live with Jon like this the rest of our lives" as opposed to, "How should we prepare for what lies further down the road?" Life will be a bit more challenging these next two weeks since Heather is taking a two-week vacation back home to Utah. Still, I sense that the rest of Jon's journey cannot be done coasting downhill. There's a fine balance between taking a breather on the flat stretches without losing the momentum for the upcoming hills. What a good and comforting feeling it is to look around and see so many supportive and loving friends and family cheering us on! I hope each one of you feels that same cheering presence as you travel your own arduous road.

May this find all of you enjoying the scenery in your life's journey – the hills as well as the valleys.

September 23, 2000; Saturday noon. *I just finished a very long, hard cry. It's been quite some time since I've needed to cry. Thank goodness the Lord provided this physical, mental, and spiritual outlet. What triggered it was seeing how impatient I was becoming with Jonathan. He's had a really rough week mentally adjusting to 1) Heather coming back from a two-week vacation, 2) Getting a new manual wheelchair with the dreaded chest harness, and 3) Touring two post-acute rehabs. Despite knowing this, I almost lost it with him. Instead, I came up to his old room and just sobbed. Eventually I found myself on my knees receiving comfort and answers from my dear Father. Again, I could picture and almost feel His arms around me. I definitely felt His love instead of reproach for my weakness. Here are some of the things we talked about....*

--Jeff is such a wonderful asset! When I am down, he is up. When I am weak, he is strong. Use him. Express my appreciation for him.

--Once again, I was reminded of what I was told from the very beginning. My greatest challenge in all of this will be enduring well to the end. Yes, I want all of this over with. Yes, I want my old life back. But, yes, Thy will be done with the right timing.

I used to be so strong! Or so I thought. Humbled, I see there is still such a long way for me to go.

October 28, 2000

Dear Friends & Family:

After slogging through a lot of delays and red tape, Jonathan's wheelchair accessible bathroom is done! I shouldn't really complain about those delays since the waiver overseen by United Disabilities Services (formerly known as UCP) paid all but $600 of the $10,000 price tag. We have been so blessed to not have the financial burden that many others go through.

We were then able to buy a Grand Caravan minivan this month which has made transporting so much easier now that we don't have to break down the wheelchair.

But the big news is that Jonathan will be living in a post-acute rehab come January 8, 2001 anywhere from 6-24 months. It's Success Rehab is in Quakertown, about one hour and 45 minutes northeast of here. (Jonathan likes to tell people he's going there because "Failure Rehab" wouldn't take him!) It's an excellent TBI rehab where he will be able to get independent living skills, vocational skills, and therapies including art and music. It's an older place in a rural setting with about 20 others living on site. He'll have his own room, share a bathroom with one other guy, and eat with most of the others. Jeff and I were most impressed by how well the staff worked together and with the residents, the upbeat atmosphere, and their progressive philosophy. After the first 30 days, visitors are always welcome, Jon can come home on special weekends, and we'll hopefully arrange for someone from the nearby LDS branch* to pick him up for church each Sunday.

How does Jon feel about all this? We didn't want to do it without his approval which he finally gave when he saw the other choices. How does the family feel about it? Both times that I have visited Success, I have been given that peaceful feeling of confirmation from the Spirit that helps me cut the apron strings and trust in these people to take care of my son. Jeff, as usual, had a bit more of a struggle letting go and yet sees the wisdom in doing so. Needless to say, the kids will miss him here in the home. Jon's presence has brought a greater peace and love into our home. Lauren will miss her cuddle time with him at night. Andrew will miss having a big brother around. And Peter will miss his chess partner. I envision a few tears, a less cluttered home, and some memorable trips up to Quakertown. It's going to be very difficult to leave family and the familiar behind, but we truly feel it is necessary for his future independence and growth.

Since his therapies at the Health Campus finished up, Jon's life has been fairly mundane. Rather than being challenged, his body is simply being maintained. The only progression are his cognitive skills, particularly his short-term memory. I know at times Jonathan gets impatient with not knowing answers to his "when" questions, such as "When will my hands work again?" "When will I be able to walk again? "When will my voice get better?" When, when, when. Funny, but the when doesn't bother me because I know that Jonathan *will* get better. Yes, I would love it sooner than later. But simply knowing that he will is really what matters. Eternally speaking, this earth life is but a dot on the never beginning/never ending time line, so it really doesn't matter! When we can get past the why and the when questions, peace of mind fills the spaces left behind in the heart and soul.

CHAPTER 25

You can call me friend
Brothers to the end
Each one's helping hand
You can call me friend

−"YOU CAN CALL ME FRIEND"
WORDS & MUSIC BY MARK RAMSDEN

January 9, 2001
Dear Friends & Family:
Today was Jonathan's first full day at Success Rehab. Needless to say, it's been a stressful, emotional, and interesting few days. Jonathan, Peter, and I made a trip to nearby Milford early Sunday morning to introduce Jon to the branch. It's a congregation of about

100 very wonderful, caring, and friendly members that quickly took Jonathan under their wing. In fact, I just got off the phone with President* Mark Ramsden who oversees the Milford Branch. He went and spent a few hours with Jonathan tonight at the Rehab. They talked music since they have the same taste and tried each other's instruments out – Pres. Ramsden's guitar and Jon's mandolin. Pres. Ramsden also had a chance to talk to some of the staff who apparently have already taken a liking to Jon and his "sage-like character." Members of the branch will be picking up Jon for church each Sunday that he is there. I have a feeling that there are some earthly angels in that small congregation prepared to provide the spiritual side of this new phase.

January 14, 2001. *How has Jonathan been this week? We've called him a few times, but don't get much other than, "I'm not sure; I don't remember." He's not begging to come home which is a good sign. In fact, I think he's pretty much accepted the fact that this is where he needs to be and will be for the next six months to two years. He still thinks the other residents are "weird," retreating to his bedroom and the computer during free time. But he is cooperative, participating, and polite.*

Did I tell you that his right hand now opens and closes? He began doing his own version of occupational therapy.

Whenever he would think about it, Jonathan would sit on that hand or lay it flat on the table, pressing it open. It's amazing that he's been able to remember to do this day after day. But it was just as amazing to see it open and working again! As far as the left hand goes, it's still tightly closed with little voluntary movement. Tendon transfer surgery can help if and when his brain can tell his hand to open up. Jonathan's usual response when told this is (looking intently at his hand), "Open, darn it! Nope, it's still not listening to my brain."

February 11, 2001. *It's been a little over a month since Jonathan moved to his "other home." He was finally able to come home last weekend. Other than looking a little too scruffy for his mother, he seemed to be doing well. He loved being with his family again, but he sorely missed his computer. In fact, he was a bit bored! Perhaps that was good since it gave him something to look forward to at the Rehab. In fact, the latest report from the psychologist said that since Jonathan came back from his weekend home, he's a lot more relaxed and even said he liked being back. I think the weekend home did his psyche some good. He now knows that we have not abandoned him and that there is still a connection to home. With that assurance, he can focus and relax a bit more. I still think he'll find his friends in the staff, but I also think he'll find a way to connect with the other residents.*

Thanks to President Ramsden, Jonathan is composing music again! Up until the week we brought the keyboard to Success, the two of them would go to the piano room and collaborate using the piano and guitar. Then Jon would go back to his room and type the lyrics. When I saw them talking together last week, I realized that Pres. Ramsden was not doing this out of duty, but that he truly enjoyed being with Jonathan. I can't help but see this simple yet significant weekly experience they have together as a sweet touch from heaven. Yes, we do have a sensitive, loving, and personal Father in Heaven!

March 21, 2001. *Here's what we've learned from the staff:*

- *They all have Jonathan's sense of humor pegged and actually appreciate it!*
- *He is in the highest of three cognitive functioning groups during the day program. Now, rather than seeing the other residents as weird and beneath him, he has something to aspire to. As Dawn put it, "Jonathan wants to be the 'top dog' here."*
- *Jonathan has gone from shunning the other residents and sneaking into his room whenever possible to participating fully, even asking other residents if they want to play a game – Scrabble and Chess being his favorite.*

- *From Jerry, the very caring and involved program administrator: "There are two Jonathans: the gifted yet uncertain Jonathan of the past and the spiritual, mature Jonathan of the future. The goal is to bring these two Jonathans together. Who knows what he will then be able to accomplish!"*

And here's what we've learned from working with the staff:

- *We as Jonathan's parents will be his best advocates. We both feel strongly that this can be done with honesty and kindness.*

- *Jonathan's journey was to include Success Rehab. We're beginning to see possible reasons why we were to choose this rehab (or a rehab at all), and continue to look forward to the answer unfolding. We continue to have strong impressions that Jonathan will improve — even to the amazement of doctors and therapists. And Jonathan will continue to touch others with his optimistic and faithful outlook. How grateful we are for the miracles and for a divinely guided journey. As Kieth Merrill said, "Our faith compels us to understand that one day, we will look back across the trials of our lives and from a celestial perspective understand precisely why things happened the way they happened." (Meridian Magazine, "The Man Who Would Be Jesus" May 5, 2000)*

July 4, 2001. *Recently, Jonathan passed a few milestones. It was two years ago June 13 that he had the accident. Just this past Monday he celebrated birthday #21. And it has been six months since we brought him to Success Rehab. Anniversaries provide the opportunity to look back and reflect. I must admit I was asking myself, "Why haven't we seen more progress at the Rehab?" That's where a loving husband with a better perspective helped me see things more clearly. He reminded me that the realistic goal of his stay there was to "fine tune" his physical and cognitive abilities, provide a setting where he could maximize his independence, and as a bonus give us a year or two respite. After talking to him, I decided to relax, sit back and watch what happens. Here's what we've recently noticed:*

- *To everyone's surprise and delight, Jonathan is actually happy living there. This change from tolerance to happiness came about the same time we noticed him reaching out to others. For example, a staff member or fellow resident will pass him in the hall and say, "Hi Jon, how are you?" Jon might reply, "I'm fine. But more importantly, how are you?" Also, I would hear more than once when he was home this past weekend, "Mom, I just want you to know how much I appreciate everything you and the family are doing for me. I love you." I guess Jonathan's heart is also being "fine tuned."*

- *Jonathan has been able to carry over from day to day a self-driven regiment of physical exercises that include sit-ups, leg lifts, and stretching now of both hands. [Author's Note: He has continued this exercise routine throughout the years that now includes sit-ups and push-ups both morning and night.] Jon can oil paint again! It finally worked out for him to take a night class at the community college where the "old ladies" love him, he and his professor talk art, and Cindy from the Rehab assists him with his needs. What a contrast his work-in-progress barn scene is to the barely readable paintings he attempted here at home. As his college friend, Erin DeSpain, put it in a recent letter, "Inside Jon's mind, there exists the mind of an artist.... His genius is still there. It was one thing that the accident could not rob from him." Perhaps Jonathan is also a "work-in-progress!"*

I'll close with sharing his birthday experiences. Jonathan ate lunch that Monday at his favorite restaurant with his favorite friend – the Taj Mahal with Melissa. I picked him up and we drove on to his friend Zach Bailey's house to spend time in his sound studio. Zach offered to create a CD using all of Jon's original compositions. We were able to hear a higher quality sound of those now precious "musical experiments."

The next night, back at the 'hab, the two young sister missionaries* from the Milford Branch put together a surprise birthday party for him at the church complete with decorations, cake, and 25 of his church friends. One of them, Sister Rumsey, called me this morning and told me that they all had a really great time. It's hard to express the love and appreciation I have for Jonathan's adopted church family. To think that these two dear Sisters would go to all the trouble to put it together, and then to have so many from the branch be there. Apparently, the Sisters visit Jonathan on a weekly basis. I'm sure it's one of the highlights of Jon's week!

November 1, 2001. *...As for an update on his physical and mental status, Jonathan is still in a wheelchair. It's not just because of weakness on his left side, but it also has to do with losing the ability to balance himself. The P.T. is hoping hippo therapy will help. No, he doesn't ride on a hippo although he would love that! Hippo apparently is the Latin word for horse. Yep, he goes to the farm once a week and rides a horse. I think he loves the setting as much as he loves the ride.*

As far as O.T. goes, Jon's left hand will now open and close when he thinks about it. This means that he is a likely candidate for tendon transfer surgery which will lengthen the tendons in his elbow and wrist. After making an appointment back in August for November 12 with a much sought after doctor in this field, we just found out that he is moving his practice to Baltimore this week. Back to square one....

Jonathan is also sitting up a little straighter and able to speak a little more clearly. Enough so that he was able to give a talk in Sacrament Meeting* two months ago. Just in case some had a hard time understanding him, they handed out copies of his talk with the program. He wrote the talk unassisted and it has his classic humor scripted in!

Jon's lack of short term memory continues to be his greatest challenge...and perhaps his greatest asset. For instance, after watching the news reports that fateful September 11, he said to one of the staff, "I can't stand to watch another building blow up" and left for his room. The next day he couldn't recall any of it happening. Unlike some of us still plagued by those horrific scenes, his mind is at peace.

To be honest, if this is as good as Jonathan gets, we will be happy for he is happy. And yet, Jon's priesthood blessings have hinted at more than this. In the meantime, Jonathan continues to light up the lives around him. I couldn't ask for more from my son!

March 5, 2002. (Excerpts from a father's letter to his son)

...Jonathan, we're excited about you going to the temple* on Thursday. We often wonder what the Lord has in store for *you.... As you think about your situation, ponder the following scripture from Hebrews 12:1: "...let us lay aside every weight, and the sin which doth so easily beset us, and let us run with patience the race that is set before us." "Race" is probably better translated into "journey" in your situation, and "run" could be reworded as "travel." You're not competing with anyone but yourself. Your goal is to travel your journey with patience, laying aside your burdens on Christ and looking to Him for your strength.*

June 23, 2002. *There are a couple of exciting things to tell you about. First of all, Jonathan is having surgery on his left foot this Wednesday. His Achilles tendon will be lengthened, hopefully making it easier to plant his foot in a normal position when walking. And we finally have a surgery date for Jon's left arm and hand – July 29. Dr. Naidu will lengthen tendons in his left wrist and hand, remove bones in the wrist for flexibility, and try Botox injections in the elbow. With both of these casts, can you imagine the stories Jonathan will come up with explaining to unsuspecting strangers just how he got in such a condition?!*

Good stuff continues to happen. What a journey this has been! And, as you can see, it's certainly not over. There is still much to learn and share. Our lives have been forever changed because of what happened to Jonathan three years ago this month. And when I say changed, I mean in such a positive, spiritual way. It's as if these experiences gave us a hefty boost up a few notches on our spiritual ladders. Sometimes it's a scary climb, but the view just keeps getting better and better!

August 20, 2002. *We're hoping to have Jonathan home by Thanksgiving! His current problem is that he is actually feeling some anxiety and fear about coming home permanently. The rehab has offered him an anchor and some significant structure in his life to hold on to. This conflict between wanting to come home and not wanting to lose his structure is evidently leading to some rebellious behavior on his part concerning his independence. He has been transferring himself out of his wheelchair on to his bed, the floor, chairs, etc. without anyone being around, and with Jon that has turned out to be a safety issue. He kind of throws himself in the general direction of where he wants to be, and when he lands there, he looks pleased with himself. He knows that he's not supposed to do this stuff, but somehow it's been fixated in his mind that everyone is holding him back, and he needs to take his own actions to make progress.*

November 24, 2002. *Jonathan is coming home for good this Tuesday, November 26! Yep, his time at "the Hab" is coming to an end. It will have been two years minus one month that, with a little fear and trepidation coupled with trust and an answer to our prayers, we let our son go. Now* with some hindsight, we can see why he needed this experience: 1) independence, 2) a set routine with great therapies, 3) experience with the Milford Branch, and 4) experience with other brain injured people. And I believe along the way Jonathan's optimistic spirit, sense of humor, and sensitivity touched others' lives. But just as we knew when it was time to let him go, we also knew it was time to bring him home. (Isn't prayer a wonderful thing!) Jonathan's lifetime waiver (government money that he qualifies for) will continue to pay for a day program here as well as attendant care for home. It looks like Acadia, the smaller brain injury rehab about 10 minutes from here, will do nicely for his day program.

Jonathan is still determined to walk. This has continued to be a major problem at the Hab with his forbidden independent transfers. (All they want to do is spot him, and yet....) We got to see this side of him when he was home for the weekend. It was just Lauren, Peter, and Jonathan home for a few hours when he crawled upstairs. Lauren somehow managed to get him up in the swivel chair and pushed him around wherever he wanted to go! Needless to say, we spotted him as he scooted down the stairs on his bum when I got home.

I'll close with The Professor's words (what the staff calls Jon at Success!) that he typed recently on the computer: "Just as peanuts often are found lodged in cookies and other such desserts, oft times people find themselves lodged into difficult situations. With myself being wedged into this rehab, I feel a lot like an almond. Or a cashew. But such desserts can sometimes taste pretty good, and I've got that a rehab could, overall, be a rewarding experience. It just takes a little adapting."

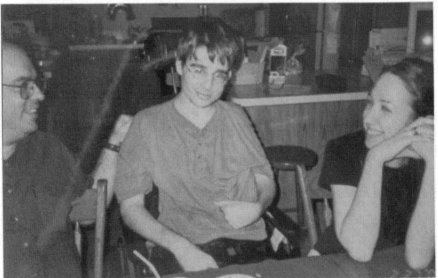

Top: Working with speech therapist Ed Woge. Bottom: Hanging out with Dad
and Melissa shortly after coming home.

Working with physical therapist Ken Fox and Marcel, the cockatiel.

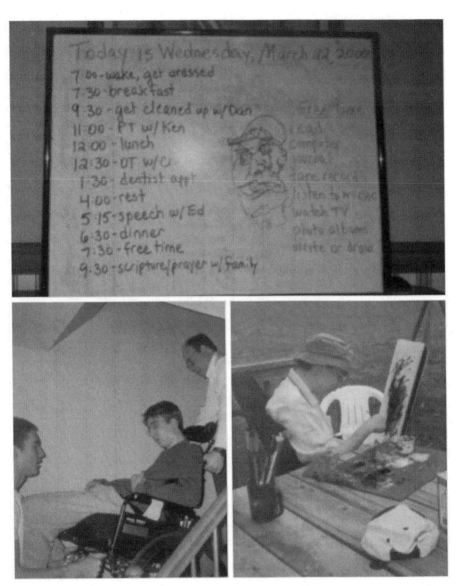

Top: Jon's schedule board where he added a drawing. Bottom left: Taking Jonathan upstairs for a shower. Bottom right: Painting for the first time after the accident.

EPILOGUE

* * *

Life has its seasons and they're all in my air
today.
>*Yes, today's the day for living and for living well,*
>*they say.*
>*For life's seasons are ever-changing and yes, its*
>*cycles do come around.*
>*And today I'm running through all of them, my*
>*footsteps on the ground,*
>*In the long run.*

>–"THE LONG RUN" WORDS BY MARK KUNKEL

I t has now been 19 years since that never-to-be-forgotten phone call. When we brought Jonathan home February 4, 2000, we had no idea just how much more he would heal. We prepared for the worst while praying for the best.

Where is he now? Jonathan, at age 38, reached a milestone this year (2018), having spent half his life with a brain injury. He continues to live with us. Thanks to the funding provided by his waiver, we were not only able to add the bathroom onto our house, but also a large bedroom/art studio as well. His siblings have married and had children. His sister lives in Idaho, but his two brothers live nearby.

What are his current disabilities? Jonathan still has difficulty remembering from one hour to the next, and even sometimes minute to minute. Fortunately, if it's important enough or repeated often enough, he *can* retain information. Afraid of losing his past, he avidly records everything. First it was a written day planner, then a Palm Pilot, and currently an I-pad. He also keeps a scrapbook and a journal.

There are other minor cognitive issues he still works on, but his brain injury seems to have affected him physically more than mentally. Like a stroke, his left side was damaged. He is now deaf in his left ear. He is blind in his left eye (except for a tiny peripheral area); thus, no depth perception. There is still weakness in his left hand, but thanks to the tendon surgery, he can do some things with it. However, his right hand is strong and usable. His left leg is weak, but significantly strengthened through his exercise regimen. He's still unable to walk, mainly due to his balance being affected, so he gets around in a wheelchair. His speech is sometimes difficult to understand.

What can he do? What can't he do? Art and music were very important to Jonathan. Although his artistic mind thinks more concrete now than abstract, he can still sketch and paint, and do it quite well thanks to assistance and mentoring from his personal care attendants with art backgrounds. Because of his physical disabilities, he's had to make adjustments. For instance, he now paints and draws with his non-dominant hand. And because of that hand's spasticity, he's learned to use larger, more fluid brush strokes and less detail. Jon celebrated his 30th birthday with his own art show at one of Lancaster's art galleries, followed by another successful one three years later. In 2017, Jonathan enjoyed returning to his alma mater, Southern Virginia University, for a show and artist talk. He continues to sell his paintings at local venues and online at aspiepathways.org.

Unfortunately, it takes two hands to play the guitar so he had to give that up. His weak and spastic hands, however, don't stop him from playing the piano, albeit at a slower, simpler pace. He still composes beautiful songs. He still sings despite his voice being hindered.

What does he do all day? Jonathan continues to go to Acadia, the brain injury rehab, two days a week for cognitive therapy. He attends Adult Enrichment, a UDS day program for adults with disabilities, another two days. Both of these programs provide him something positive to do with his time, art and music classes that he loves, and an outlet for new friends.

Through his personal care attendant hours, he is also able to be active in the community. He goes to the YMCA twice a week where he swims, works out with the equipment, or walks around with his walker. (He's certainly making up for his lack of sports and exercise before the accident!) For many years, his calling* in the church was typing up the weekly Sunday bulletin. He now co-teaches a Primary class of 7-year-olds.

What is Jonathan known for? His quick wit. His easy going, upbeat nature and positive outlook. His thoughtfulness and gratitude. And he's very willing to share his story in the hopes that it will help someone else.

What does he like to do? Besides art and music, he loves to write stories. He loves to play games on his computer and I-pad. He loves to tie unusual knots for his Sunday ties – and watch the videos that go along with them. He likes to play board games and put together puzzles. And he loves to hang out with his friends and family.

* * *

Brain injuries can affect its victims in so many different ways -- behavior, personality, intelligence, cognition, or physical disabilities -- just depending upon the areas affected. I've yet to hear the injury *fixing* a part of the brain. But that is exactly what happened with Jonathan and his *mentally* broken brain. His bi-polar illness simply went away and has never come back. When asked which he would rather deal with – the TBI or the depression – Jonathan will tell you the TBI. Why? Because he can be himself without that constant dark cloud hovering over him. Yes, there are days he gets frustrated with his current disabilities, but his natural easy-going nature and sense of humor help him get through these times.

As you can see, so does his faith. Faith in God provides hope that there will be complete healing --- if not in this life then in the hereafter. Faith provides answers. Will Jonathan marry? Will he be a father? Because of God's plan, we know that yes, he will have those opportunities – again, if not in this life then in the life to come. Faith provides peace of mind and frees us to enjoy life as it is.

Have we as a society, as God's children, forgotten to be faithful? Are we teaching our children to believe? For without that belief, they can and are struggling to cope with life's difficulties. We have seen a number of families fall apart in crises similar to ours because they did not believe. They did not know that they could call upon God and He could bring them peace, understanding, and even healing. Relationships with both God and family are essential to weather the storms of life. And not just to survive, but to end up stronger and more beautiful because of these storms.

"Emerging Artist" Show at Red Raven Gallery 2010

Art Show at Mulberry Art Studio 2013

Visiting Southern Virginia's art room in 2015

With friend Leslie Daubert 2016

Building frame with personal care attendant/art teacher Karin Wengenroth 2016

Giving the artist talk at SVU Exhibition 2017

Whitlock Family 2017
Peter, Annette, Jonathan, Jeff, Andrew, Lauren

To hear the song "The Long Run" sung and played by Jonathan, to view the paintings and photos in color, and to see more of Jonathan's artwork, go to JonathanWhitlockArt.com.

GLOSSARY OF
MORMON* TERMS

* * *

(For more information, go to mormon.org)

A

Atonement – Like grace, refers to the sacrifice Jesus made in the Garden of Gethsemane as well as on the cross so that we can be forgiven of our sins. We can then live again in God's presence, having been made perfect through Jesus Christ.

B

Bishop – Ecclesiastical leader of a congregation. The LDS church is a lay ministry, including the bishop.

Book of Mormon – Like the Holy Bible, the Book of Mormon is God's dealings with His children who have been taught the gospel of Jesus Christ. While the Bible takes place in the Old World, the Book of Mormon takes place in the New World from about 600 BC – 400 AD. We believe that both the Bible and the Book of Mormon are the word of God.

Branch – A smaller LDS congregation than a ward. The ecclesiastical leader of a branch is called "President."

C

Callings – Being a lay ministry provides opportunities for all members of the congregation to take on assignments. These assignments are callings prayerfully considered and given by the leaders of the stake or ward.

D

Doctrine & Covenants – Part of the LDS canon of scripture that also includes the Bible, the Book of Mormon, and the Pearl of Great Price. As our ninth "Article of Faith" states, "We believe all that God has revealed, all that He does now reveal, and we believe that He will yet reveal many great and important things pertaining to the Kingdom of God."

E

Elders – How we refer to male missionaries instead of using their first names, e.g. Elder Smith.

Ensign – The church magazine for adults.

F

Family Home Evening – Monday evenings are set aside each week for LDS families to gather for gospel instruction, fun, and refreshments.

Fast – To go without food and drink voluntarily for a certain period of time and with a spiritual purpose in mind. The first Sunday of each month is designated a day to fast, but members can fast any time they wish.

G

Girls Camp – Or Young Women's Camp. An annual event of camping for girls ages 12-18 and their leaders.

M

Millennium – LDS doctrine shares the Christian doctrine that Jesus Christ will come again and reign on this earth for a thousand years. There will be no sickness, no pain, no disabilities.

Mission – Although not required, every young man looks forward to the age where they can go and serve a proselyting mission for two years. In 1999, that age was 19. They do not choose where they go. Rather, it is done by revelation through the church's Missionary Council in Salt Lake City, Utah. Mission papers are sent in prior to the call, with the young man's information on it.

Missionaries – Young adults, both men and women, can serve a proselyting mission – two years for young men called "Elders" and 18 months for young women called "Sisters." They pay their own way and are called by inspiration anywhere throughout the world and the United States.

Mormon – Shortened nickname for members of The Church of Jesus Christ of Latter-day Saints. Also referred to as Latter-day Saints (LDS).

Moses 1:39 – An excerpt from a book in the LDS canon of scripture called the Pearl of Great Price. The verse is a response by God to Moses with the entire verse reading, "For behold, this is my work and my glory – to bring to pass the immortality and eternal life of man."

Mutual – The church's activity night for youth ages 12-18.

N

New Era – The church magazine for youth 12-18 years of age.

P

Premortal life – Our existence as spirit beings in the presence of God before we were born.

Priesthood blessing – The Priesthood is the power and authority to act in the name of Jesus Christ here on earth. Given that authority, men in the church are then able to lay their hands on the sick and afflicted and provide words and healing from God. Others can also be given blessings of comfort or guidance.

President Ezra Taft Benson – Prophet and President of The Church of Jesus Christ of Latter-day Saints from 1985-1994.

Primary – The church's organization for children ages 18 months through 11 years that meets for two hours on Sundays following Sacrament Meeting.

R

Relief Society – The women's organization of the church, of which all women ages 18 and older are members.

S

Sacrament Meeting – The first of a three-hour block of Sunday meetings that includes partaking of the Lord's sacrament. After the sacrament, talks are given by selected members of the congregation.

Seminary – A scripture study class for LDS high school students that meets prior to their school day.

Sisters – What we often call women in the church, reminding us that, because we are all God's children, we then are brothers and sisters to one another. It is also used instead of female missionaries' first name, e.g. Sister Radmall.

Stake – A larger unit of the church, created from 5–12 wards and branches that are found in the same geographic area.

T

Temple – Like temples in the Bible, modern day LDS temples are literally houses of the Lord where sacred ordinances take place and the Spirit can provide guidance and peace.

Testimony – Bearing witness publicly of the gospel tenets we believe to be true. Typically, the first Sunday of the month's Sacrament Meeting (the same day designated to fast two meals) is the meeting set aside for members of the congregation to voluntarily stand at the pulpit and bear their testimonies.

The Friend – The church magazine for children up to age 12.

W

Ward – The name of a large Mormon congregation (smaller ones being called branches). The ward we attend has about 150 attending church each Sunday.

Washington Temple – Located in a suburb of Washington D.C., about two hours away, it is one of over 150 LDS temples found throughout the world.

Y

Young Women – The church program for girls 12-18 years of age. They meet during the third hour of the Sunday block of meetings and during Mutual. At the time of the accident, I had been called, or assigned, to be the President of the organization.

ACKNOWLEDGMENTS

* * *

Thank you to my readers: Daughter-in-law Rachel Whitlock who took a swipe at the first draft. Cousin Marianne Carter whose encouraging words kept me going. Coworker Cathy Strawser who encouraged me to broaden my audience. My dad, Mel Montgomery, who read for grammar with a fine-toothed comb and set a wonderful example of self-publishing. And my English major friends Sherma Woolstenhulme and Ruth Turner who provided confidence and expertise.

Thank you to my husband Jeff who handled the technical side of it. What would I do without you (in so many ways).

Made in the USA
Middletown, DE
26 August 2018